THE FIELDS

THE FIELDS

Our Journey through Medicine, Mission, Life, and Faith

Manh Dang, MD

ELM HILL

A Division of
HarperCollins Christian Publishing

www.elmhillbooks.com

The Fields
Our Journey through Medicine, Mission, Life, and Faith

Published in Nashville, Tennessee, by Elm Hill, an imprint of Thomas Nelson. Elm Hill and Thomas Nelson are registered trademarks of HarperCollins Christian Publishing, Inc.

Elm Hill titles may be purchased in bulk for educational, business, fund-raising, or sales promotional use. For information, please e-mail SpecialMarkets@ ThomasNelson.com.

The cover photo is a license free image by Daniel Reche from Pixabay.

Library of Congress Cataloging-in-Publication Data

Library of Congress Control Number: 2019915671

ISBN 978-1-400327768 (Paperback)
ISBN 978-1-400327775 (HardBound)
ISBN 978-1-400327782 (eBook)

TABLE OF CONTENTS

CHAPTER 3 – THE MISSION FIELD

CHAPTER 4 – GOD'S MASTERPIECES, THE FIELD OF GRACE

CHAPTER 5 – HEAVEN AND EARTH, THE FIELD OF BLESSINGS

CHAPTER 6 – THE FIELD OF TRUTH

CHAPTER 7 – VALLEYS AMONG THE FIELDS

CHAPTER 8 – THE MEDICAL FIELD

CHAPTER 9 – MY HOME FIELD

FOREWORD

“It has been my privilege to know, and serve alongside, Dr. Manh Dang as his Pastor and friend for more than twenty years. When my family moved to Huntsville, AL in 1996 to plant a new church, his lovely wife, Karen was a key member of our original core team. It was several months later, at the baptism of their triplet boys, when Manh attended a service at our new church for the first time. This marked the beginning of a spiritual journey for him that has not only been life changing for him, but to many others he has impacted along the way.

Rarely, if ever, have I encountered a more kind and gentle soul. As a Medical Oncologist, Dr. Dang exhibits an empathy and compassion for his patients that is fueled and enhanced by his deep faith. In addition to his vocational work, Manh has dedicated his life to demonstrating God's love to people in some of the poorest places in the world. He has tirelessly devoted his time, talent and treasure to partner with various Christ-centered missions, particularly in Kenya and the Dominican Republic.

Over the past several years, Manh's friends and followers on social media have marveled at the heartfelt eloquence of his inspirational posts. Many of us have urged him to consider publishing a compilation of these posts in book form, so a wider audience could benefit from their wisdom. Manh's humility made him reluctant to do so. But persistence paid off and you, the readers, are the beneficiaries.

The honest reflections contained in these pages come from a very deep place. Manh writes from his experiences as a Christian, physician, missionary, husband, father, and friend. He immigrated to the United States as a child, with his family of origin, during the height of the Vietnam War. This gives him a unique perspective and love for our country and the freedoms we enjoy, but often take for granted.

Finally, it came as no surprise to me that the proceeds from this book will benefit mission causes close to Manh's heart around the world. I pray you will be as blessed as I have been by these writings. And may you be doubly blessed by knowing that, in doing so, you are helping to share God's love with others in need.

Rev. John W. Tanner,
Lead Pastor, Cove Church
Huntsville, AL"

DISCLAIMER AND DISCLOSURE

If this book has any flaws, it is because I am very flawed as a person and as an untrained writer. If it has any redeeming quality, you can bet it all comes from above. Though the subject matters discussed in this book can be serious, I hope the message is always encouraging, uplifting, honoring or reflective, truthful, and not meant to be condemning. The opinions expressed are my own and not representations of any organization that I work with. I am currently living in the beautiful state of Alabama, USA, so my observation reflects its flavor but I believe our whole world is a beautiful place despite the constant lurking of evil. The names of my patients and their family members who inspired me to write in their honor have been changed to protect their privacy. The entirety of the proceeds from the sale of this book, no matter how big or small, will be donated to the Russell Hill Cancer Foundation to aid poor or uninsured cancer patients in our community and to the ministries that I have the blessing of witnessing their incredible impacts locally and globally for the Kingdom, which I will list below. God bless you all!

Desert Rose Ministries by Teresa June Estes
desertroseministries.com
Until They Know Ministry by Brad Jenkins
untiltheyknow.org
Kenya Relief by Steve James and with Curtis and Devry Coghlan
kenyarelief.org
coghlansinkenya.com
Bessong & Ministries by Chaplain Bessie White
Project Abundant Life by Steve and Leigh Willhelm

INTRODUCTION

"**B**rothers, what we do in life echoes in eternity," the Roman general says, shattering the eerie silence that precedes the storm. In the opening scene of the movie *Gladiator* (2000) directed by Ridley Scott, there is a close-up of a man's hand skimming and carefully touching the top of the crop as he walks through a wheat field. The reflection of golden sunlight on the field, the swaying of the wheat stalks by a gentle breeze, and the chirping of song birds from a distance denote a leisurely walk of a farmer who cherishes the simple things in life. The next scene is a dramatic contrast showing the protagonist, a Roman general named Maximus (Russell Crowe), intensely staring at the black forest where a barbaric tribe of Germania lurks. To prepare his troops for the inevitable battle ahead, Maximus mounts his horse and rides to the front to proclaim the aforementioned truth—"What we do in life echoes in eternity"—and to remind the battle-fatigued Roman legions the image of home where they long to return to once the fight is over, he urges on: "Imagine where you will be and it will be so." What follows next is a brief but brutal and bloody clash of epic proportion on a cold and dark day between two mortal enemies that results in victory for the Roman conquerors and eventually brings peace to the empire.

To reward Maximus for this heroic conquest, the ailing Roman Emperor Marcus Aurelius (Richard Harris) appoints him, whom he loves and trusts more than anyone else, the regent of Rome and bypasses Aurelius' own son Commodus (Joaquin Phoenix), the cowardly and evil antagonist. Burning with anger and jealousy, Commodus assassinates Aurelius, Maximus' wife and young son, and orders the murder of Maximus to become the tyrannical ruler of the Roman empire. The movie continues with Maximus escaping death but severely wounded, rescued and sold as a slave to become a gladiator in Roman arenas. For the rest of this captivating historical drama, through toils and battles, Maximus' singular purpose in life is to survive and avenge the death of his emperor, his family, and to help return Rome to a republic and to free it from the brutal, oppressive control of his antagonist.

For most of us, our lives are a little like that of Maximus', who at heart is a peaceful farmer, but the circumstances of his life forces him to stand up against the evil of the day and fights not just for his survival but for what he loves most and what he believes is morally right. For most of us, our lives are intermingled series of peaceful walks in the "fields" with our loved ones and battles for survival, whether they come from the dark forests of poverty, losses, rejection, abandonment, abuse, or illnesses of all shapes and forms.

This book is a compilation of my short Facebook posts over the last few years aimed primarily to encourage my family and friends as well as myself in our life struggles, and as an oncologist, to uplift those of us out there who are fighting cancer and other devastating illnesses and to honor those who succumbed from their courageous battles. I also hope that reading this book will remind us all that oftentimes in life, the most beautiful things are the most simple ones and they are also the most precious gifts from above. Some of my writings are fictional but many are about the people whom I am blessed to share or have shared my life journey with. Some are my real-life heroes who shine brightly as they stand and face their "Commodus." Some have defeated their foes and some did not but in God's arena, I believe all of them were victorious. Some are at the forefront of another field, the mission field to care for and share the love of God with the least amongst us. They too, are fighting for survival, not just for themselves but for those who can't.

The good news is no matter how difficult our battles in life are, God has already sent His son Jesus to fight and die for our eventual salvation. Victory has already been proclaimed. We just have to stand and face our nemesis, the Prince of Darkness, on earth until the day we can walk with God in His field in heaven. In the meantime, while walking through the fields of life, we should strive to live well, love well, do well, and fight well if we must because "what we do in life echoes in eternity." Another simple truth is God, whom we'll walk with some day in His field of eternity, will not abandon us as we walk through our fields of life on earth.

CHAPTER 1

THE FIELD'S FOUR SEASONS

Autumn in the South

The heat is lifted and the crisp, cool air finally returns to Alabama this autumn. There is something about the sights and sense of autumn that warms the hearts of even the worst critics among us.

Perhaps it is the rich colors of the changing leaves that remind us of the immeasurable beauty of God's creation. From radiant yellow to warm orange to majestic red, the pigments of autumn leaves evoke in us the deepest sense of awe and appreciation of the best Artist of all.

Perhaps it is the early morning mist over the fields, the tiny droplets of dew on farmers' crops that are yet to be harvested, and the calls of the Canadian geese flying south that signal in many of us the arrival of the favorite season of the year.

Perhaps it is the formations of the clouds, the freshness of the rains that cleanse the busy streets and the dancing of the falling leaves that are caught up by the swirling winds that display the miracles of fall and remind us also that Halloween and Thanksgiving are just around the corner.

Or perhaps it is the sky at dusk that showcases the brilliant colors of heaven before darkness descends, as if the angels holding lanterns to check on the Master's children coming home from work, to make sure we're safe before tucking us in with His heavenly blanket.

Or perhaps it is the grocery stores that are aglow with the many varieties of luscious apples, delectable gourds, corns and pumpkins, and the aroma of cinnamon and freshly made apple ciders nestled among aisles of goods that excite the shoppers with the sentiment of fall.

Or is it the aroma of home-cooked meals and desserts from mom, the fall decorations that adorn the kitchens and dining tables, the return of children from wayward schools, the togetherness of family sharing foods and laughters, and especially in the South, college football that make this season oh so special?

Fall is also a season of nostalgia, both of good and bad. For those of us who are older, the holiday season can heighten the sense of loss— loss of health or fortune or of loved ones.

And like any other season, it can be a time of tragedy and hurricane Michael that devastated the Florida panhandle (in October 2018) is a stark example of that.

But fall, for us and many around the world, is uniquely the season of thanksgiving. It reminds us that amid life's struggles, the bounty that we have is nothing short of blessings from above. God is with us in all seasons and "every good and perfect gift is from above, coming down from the Father of the heavenly lights." He is with us this autumn. He is with us in the heat of the summers, the promise of the springs, and the freezing cold of the winters. He is with us, especially when life is hard.

Let's enjoy our autumn in the South or anywhere else in the world! Let's not allow our differences, especially our political views, to separate us. Let's declare our rights at the voting booths and not at each other's face. Let's look to lift each other up and not just work to promote our own wellbeing. Let's watch our tongues whether in spoken words or writings on social media as it is God's will to unite and not divide us. So let's praise God for His amazing grace and sovereign will today. And let's gather with family and friends to share some good foods and laughters and watch college football. Happy autumn everyone!

Image by Shirley Hirst from Pixabay

"Rejoice in the Lord your God, for He has given you the autumn rains because He is faithful."

– JOEL 2:23, NIV

December in the South

The difference between life and death is only one heartbeat but an ocean of joy or sorrow.

The difference between love and hate is one emotion but a lifetime of bliss or turmoil.

The difference between darkness and light is just an instance but from them one can be lost or found.

The difference between doubt and faith is often small but one tends to imprison and the other one frees.

Life is full of the little things but it's the little things that make life grand. Let's embrace and cherish the little things. It is through the little things that God orchestrates His great plans.

Though my heart may ache this season for the people I lost, I do thank God for every moment that I had with them. From each one I learned to appreciate life amid suffering, feel love in a world full of resentment, see light more clearly in dark hallways, and have stronger faith despite moments of doubt. For those of us who are missing our loved ones or the people we cared for who recently passed, remember also that life on earth is like a December morning mist that when it fades, it also reveals a field of the evergreens over the horizon.

"Be faithful in small things because it is in them that your strength lies"

– Mother Teresa

On The Sides of
The Freeway

Driving on the freeways of our nation this spring, travelers are treated with a display of wildflowers sprinkling the medians or the sides of the roads. Like a Norman Rockwell painting, the springtime blooms in glorious colors promise sojourners an exciting adventure ahead or reaffirm to homeward bound drivers that home is ultimately where the heart always longs to return to.

Uncultivated, unmanicured, unplanned and wild by our earthly standard, but these flowers could be God's artistic reminder that beauty often comes naturally and unexpectedly. Most of us won't know what they are, but ask a botanist and we'll be amazed as to the variety of the wild blooms canvassing the fields and the hills of our countryside. Just in Alabama, for example, one can spot azalea, bluebell, buckeye, and buttercup at the beginning of the botanical alphabet all the way to trout lily, and violet at its end. And even within Alabama, the locations and soil conditions will determine which particular species will thrive.

Going through life is a little like driving on the freeway. In the hustle and bustle of our days, we can completely miss the good and the beauty around us until one day, when we realize they're no longer here. Or we can slow down a bit and take the time to appreciate the gift a moment can bring. We should cherish and give thanks to those who bless us with their love, time, or gifts and do so now rather than later. Let them know they are each a precious part of our journey and not mere randomness on the fringes of life. Just like the wild flowers on the sides of the freeway, they are part of God's design for our lives and they may not be here tomorrow. Give thanks to God also for those who trouble or even torment us, for they may also be a part of God's desire for our journeys. We might be the "flowers" that they need to see. If not, they might be the "fertilizer" for our own growth.

The next time I see wild flowers on the sides of a freeway, I will try to remember the blessings that God bestows on me, including the people that were, are, and will be placed in my life and praise Him for His grace. And finally, there is nothing more beautiful than the love He has for me and you through Jesus our Savior. His love is neither annual nor perennial but everlasting. The grass may wither and flowers may fall, but His word and His love endure forever.

"The grass withers and the flowers fall, but the word of our God endures forever."

– ISAIAH 40:8, NIV

Morning Glories

Morning glories are annual flowering vines. They are "twining climbers" that will wind their ways up on any supporting structure next to them. They belong to the Convovulaceae family, a word originating from Convolvere which means to climb in Latin. There are at least 50 genera and 1000 species in the Convovulaceae family but all morning glories produce beautiful trumpet-shaped blossoms in various brilliant colors that contrast with the lush green heart-shaped foliage. These plants flourish in full sun and as the name goes, the flowers open up with all their glory and effervescence in the early dawn and close up in the afternoon. They produce a faint and pleasant fragrance. I read that gardeners like them because they are easy to grow, fast growing, and will thrive in poor, dry soils and can reseed themselves. They will attract butterflies and hummingbirds when they bloom from early summer to the first frost. Their characteristic beauty and grace make them a popular choice as decorating plants against walls or fences. One of the most popular variety of morning glories is the "Heavenly Blue." How magnificent it must feel to sit under a magnolia tree in a garden one Alabama late summer morning, to sip on a glass of sweet ice tea and admire the harmony of butterflies and humming birds flirting with morning glory on the fence.

America used to be one nation under God. Lately, we feel more like a divided country. We build invisible fences to separate us from each other along racial, gender, economic, political, and other social divides. Many universities, celebrities, the media, and especially politicians are all culpable for promoting this division either due to their own biases or for their own agenda. Some of us legitimized our own positions by calling those with an opposing view names often ending in -phobic or -ist or worse. The recent cycles of presidential elections were probably the most divisive ones in our nation's history and emotional wounds still run deep. But it's time for us to heal. It's time to bind these wounds and bridge the many divides. Continuation of insulting or incendiary remarks do nothing for the healing process. Though it's within one's right to protest, it's not lawful to cause public destruction or harm to innocent bystanders. College students need to get off the "safe zones" where they can cower under the protection against "emotional pain" and go where real pains are. This week, there will be children near our communities who won't have enough to eat. Today, there are children somewhere dying from cancer and more resources are needed for research to find better treatments. Today, there are hotbeds in Alabama and in almost every state of the nation where sex trafficking is thriving and tonight, there are homeless veterans looking for food in the dumpsters and sleep under a bridge. Tonight, some kids in inner cities across the nation will die from drug-related homicides. Go there and you'll see real pain. Go there and there are causes worth working for.

We shouldn't depend on our government or even our churches to heal our emotional wounds. That responsibility comes from each one of us. Make an effort to reach out to those different from us and find a common cause to work on. Like the morning glory, we can climb any fence or wall that separates us and make our world better for everyone. Focus more on our commonality than on our differences. Learn to listen to each other's plight and try to carry each other's burden. We are each other's neighbor and one of God's greatest commandments is to love one another. May God bless and help heal our nation! May all glory be to God, morning or night!

Image by Angeles Balaguer from Pixabay

"Love your neighbor as yourself."

– MARK 12:31, NIV

CHAPTER 2

THE FIELD'S HOLIDAYS

Letters from Mom
(Mother's Day)

Mother's Day is around the corner and this story illustrates a timeless mother's love. My memory of her forever lives in my consciousness since I met this woman almost twenty years ago. It was in my early years of practicing oncology in Huntsville, Alabama. She was in her early thirties, newlywed, and was pregnant when she was referred to see us for breast cancer. We managed to get her through chemotherapy then surgery before she gave birth to a beautiful daughter. Unfortunately, not long after her daughter was born, my patient showed signs of recurrence, and this time with metastatic disease. Evil had come back with an angry vengeance. After failing a series of chemotherapy and radiation treatment, I put her on a chemotherapy drug that I thought would be unlikely to work, but that's the only drug I hadn't tried. By some miracle, the tumor relented this time and loosened its grip, at least for a couple of years. She ultimately succumbed to the menacing disease shortly after celebrating her daughter's second birthday. After her death, I learned that she spent the two years not just enduring the toxicity of radiation and chemotherapy, but also writing heartfelt letters to her daughter! Until the daughter was old enough to read these letters, she had instructed her husband to read them at the appropriate times. There was a letter for the first day of kindergarten, one for first grade, one for sweet sixteen, one on her first date, one for the high school prom, one for the wedding day, and so on. Even when she fought to stay alive, my patient prepared for her death and she prepared to be a part of her daughter's life long after she was to depart this earth. The letters apparently expressed maternal wisdom and most of all, motherly love.

I don't know what were written in these letters. They were private between her and her daughter. I, however, knew her heart. Helping her to fight the cancer battle for over two years, even before her daughter was born and having heart to heart discussions with her many times on many things including life and death, I believe I knew her heart and if I'm to guess at the essence of her letters, it would be something like this:

My daughter, even though I'm no longer physically here, my love for you is everlasting.

Though my spirit is heaven bound, my love for you will be evident every time these letters are read.

Until I see you again, my essence is alive in each and every word in these letters.

Until I see you again, my maternal wisdom in these letters will be the light that will shine on your path.

Though my arms can no longer hold you, I hope you know even death cannot keep my love from you.

Every time you are lonely, open these letters and I will be there with you.

When you are overjoyed, open them to remind you that I also rejoice with you in heaven.

And when your tears overflow and my words look blurry, it is because I, too, will cry with you.

Though my heart no longer beats, the love that it pours out for you will be at your fingertips every time your hands hold one of these letters.

There will be a time that you will see me again and I will personally tell you that there is nothing that could separate my love from you. Until that day comes, these letters will remind you of my promise to always love you.

It has been close to twenty years and the young girl now is a young woman. I hope she knows how blessed she is. I hope she knows that her life is covered with an undying love from a mother who, in death, chose to be alive in the words she penned.

God's love for us transcends the limit of space and time. Romans 8:38 describes His love as such.

God created us in His image and since God is love, we are therefore reflections of His love and I cannot think of any love on earth purer than that of a mother's for her children. Mothers are creatures that reflect God's quality most radiantly and on this Mother's Day, we should lift up and honor all mothers out there and thank them for many things, but most importantly for the love they have for their children. Their love can and does transcend the limit of space and time.

Happy Mother's Day!

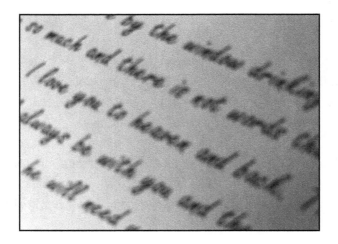

"For I am convinced that neither death nor life, neither angels nor demons, neither the present nor the future, nor any powers, neither height nor depth, nor anything else in all creation, will be able to separate us from the love of God that is in Christ Jesus our Lord."

– ROMANS 8:38, NIV

THE BEAUTY IN HIM
(Christmas)

The beauty in Him is that He did not come to take but to give. He could have been born in a king's palace but chose an animal dwelling and an unwed peasant Jewish girl. He who created heavens and earth came not to destroy but to save. He who holds the stars in his hands and has legions of angels by his feet came not to condemn but to be condemned for our sins. He who came from the highest of places came not to be worshiped but to wash the feet of the lowlife sinners like me. He who could have wiped the slate clean and started all over but chose to be mocked, whipped, and killed to salvage a greedy and petulant human race. He who in human form shook with fear in a garden one cold and dark night, but asked to do His Father's will. To me, His beauty is not always initially seen but is always eventually felt and His beauty taught me not to always dwell on my personal struggles but strive to be of service to others. The most beautiful part in Him is He came because He loved—the love that does not boast, nor envy, nor keep record of wrongs and the love that is not easily excitable but patient and kind; the love that does not delight in evil but always seeks truth. The beauty in Him is unfading and timeless and I'm grateful that His beauty does not seek to expose my ugliness but to outshine it. And the most amazing part about Jesus' beauty is He came not only to save but to make us His friends! Happy birthday, dear friend!!!

Image by Annalise Batista from Pixabay

"Love is patient, love is kind. It does not envy, it does not boast, it is not proud. It does not dishonor others, it is not self-seeking, it is not easily angered, it keeps no record of wrongs. Love does not delight in evil but rejoices with the truth. It always protects, always trusts, always hopes, always perseveres."

– 1 CORINTHIANS 13:4–7, NIV

WHEN THIS MORNING COMES
(New Year)

When this morning comes, the early dawn signals the beginning of a new year. Like any other year, this past one was full of many wonderful memories and some that we would gladly leave behind. For some of us, it was the year that we experienced the most painful losses, and last year was forever seared in our hearts. But every year is a gift and as we get older time does seem to accelerate and the gift of life is moving on ever faster. Like a roller coaster, life can be turbulent with many sudden turns and ups or downs. It can be frightening, surprising, and out of our control but also exhilarating. On this new year morning, I think of those who lost so much or sacrificed so dearly this past year and I am grateful for what were given in years past and accepting what was taken away and embrace what's to come in the new year with a heart of gratitude, because every year is a gift from God. Happy New Year to my family and friends! May today and every day of your life this year be filled with hope, joy and love, and abundant blessings from above!

"Resolve to keep happy, and your joy and you shall form an invisible host against difficulties."

– Helen Keller

"You are never too old to set another goal or to dream a new dream."

– C.S. Lewis

If Our Flag Could Speak
(Memorial Day)

I am the American flag. I stand for one nation under God. I am the embodiment of life, liberty, and the pursuit of happiness.

I am white because I stand for justice. I am blue because the sky is the limit of opportunities in America, if you're willing to work hard for them. But I am red because I am bought with a great price—the price of blood from generations of men and women who fought for me, and my stars are to commemorate their gallantry.

I've been around the block a few times. I withstood the British bombardment at Fort McHenry with my defenders during the dawn of this great nation. I was planted in the sands of Iwo Jima, the shores of Tripoli, the beach of Normandy, the rice paddies of Korea, the jungles of Vietnam, the bombed out buildings of Fallujah and the mountains of Afghanistan by our brave servicemen and women.

My greatest pride is being carried to battles by the nation's sons and daughters who come from different walks of life but united by the love for each other and for this great nation.

My greatest honor is to drape over the bodies of the fallen heroes coming home from having made the ultimate sacrifice.

I am often used as a prop behind politicians as they make their speeches and displayed on the hoods of the head-of-state motorcade. But I'm most honored when I'm flown at an American outpost in a distant land.

I'm a little flag painted on the tail of Air Force One but I am held with highest regard in an American Humvee as it entered a street rigged with enemy's IEDs.

I feel at home in the hands of an American soldier when he kneels and prays before he rises to make a stand. And I'm finally home when I'm neatly folded and handed over to the hands of his widow or mother.

I show no anger to those who trampled on me or desecrated me on our nation's streets as I forgave them for their ingratitude and ignorance.

But I have no regards for those who show up at a soldier's funeral to stage a war protest as their depravity is too much to bear.

I am seen everywhere at the Fourth of July and on this day, the Memorial Day, but where I really want to be seen is at the grave sites of the ones who sacrificed for me, including the tombs of the unknown soldiers.

So when you see me on this Memorial Day, take a moment to bow your heads and thank your God for the freedom you have and thank the men and women of the American armed forces who fought and died to gain and to preserve it. I am the American flag.

"God bless America, land that I love. Stand beside her, and guide her through the night with a light from above."

– Irving Berlin

MOTHER'S LOVE
(Mother's Day)

Do you remember, as a child, waking up on Saturday mornings to the mouthwatering aroma of freshly baked biscuits in the oven and enticing sights and sounds of breakfast as your mother was stooping over the kitchen stove preparing it? Do you remember opening your eyes as your fever broke and saw the face of an angel with sleepy eyes, smiling and tenderly caressing your hair? Do you remember sitting in the living room and your mother turned around with a disappointed look after just talking to your teacher on the phone and knowing the punishment to come would hurt her more than it would hurt you? Do you remember seeing her quietly sobbing as she went about her business and realizing that you just did or said something that broke her heart? Do you remember, in your cap and gown, receiving the diploma and looking down at the audience and catching a glimpse of your mother's tears? Do you remember seeing the same tears as you said good bye to start a family of your own? And for most of the ladies out there, she is or was your best friend, your confidant, your fashion adviser as you know her opinion is what you would value most and of course, the shoulder you cried on when your own heart was broken. And for the gentlemen, she is or was the sunshine in the morning and the North Star in the night. Our mothers' love is deeper than the deepest ocean, taller than the highest peak, gentler than the summer breeze, richer than the colors of the autumn leaves, purer than the early winter snow, and more fragrant than cherry blossoms in springtime. Though the seasons of our lives and theirs may change, their love for us never does.

Just like anybody else, the memories of my mother live in the deepest part of my soul, and my love for her dwells in the most special place in my heart. She taught me many things including my first English phrases not long after she learned them herself. But what I learn most from her, who was a devout Buddhist, is to be compassionate and to respect all people and all things that God created. I remember seeing her tears from the rearview mirror as I drove away to start my career away from home. I remember seeing the same tears many years later as I held her hands for the last time and was reminded then that her love for me was one of the only few permanent fixtures in my life. I remember being gripped with both love and sadness as I held her close one more time before I scattered her ashes into the water below and returned her to God.

Yes our mothers may not be perfect, but the love they have for us is. On this Mother's Day, for those of us who are fortunate enough to still have our mothers, let's cherish and celebrate them and shower them with our time and gifts and more importantly, our love. For those whose mothers are now in heaven, let's remember and honor them also with the only thing that can transcend life and death—our love in return. Happy Mother's Day to all!

"What is a mom but the sunshine of our days and the North Star of our nights?"

– Robert Breault

HERO

(Fourth of July)

A young man graduated from high school less than two months ago and turned seventeen a few days afterward. As a birthday and a graduation gift, his mother bought him a first class airfare to fly from Huntsville, Alabama, to see his dad in Virginia on this special day, the Independence Day. He could have chosen to go anywhere, but seeing his dad on the 4th of July was his wish. As he settled in his comfortable seat of the Boeing 747, giddy with the prospect of first class service and amenities, he watched a long line of passengers passing by to go to their seats designed for the "commoners." But one particular passenger caught his eyes. He was in his late sixties, struggling to go through the aisle as a double amputee with prosthetic legs, tall, and a bit scraggy, carrying an old Army duffel bag. By his attire, wearing a green beret and a biker jacket decorated with medals, the young man could tell he was a Vietnam veteran. The old gentleman maneuvered to his coach seat, put up his bag in the overhead bin, and with great difficulty, sat down with his prosthetic legs almost to his chest as there wasn't enough leg room.

A few moments later, as the plane was about to take off, the young man approached the veteran and asked, "Sir, would you like to trade seat with me?"

"Uh … sure, you don't like your seat?" the old vet replied.

"It's okay, but I think you would like it better, as my seat has more leg room, not to mention the gourmet meal and all the spirits you can have sure beat the stale bag of peanuts any day," the young man replied, chuckling.

"Oh, thank you, but son, you don't have to do that," the old man said, smiling.

"It would be my honor, sir. Besides, I'm not hungry and I'm under-age for the alcoholic beverages anyway," the young man insisted.

"OK then, you may regret this," the old man nodded with appreciation.

The plane landed in Reagan National Airport a few hours later. The young man deplaned and as he was heading to the baggage claim area, the veteran stood waiting to thank him. "It's so nice of you, young man, for showing pity on an old vet like me. Thank you!""

"It's not pity, sir! It's gratitude for your service to our country" was the reply.

"Is your dad going to meet you here?" the veteran asked as he lifted the duffel bag to his shoulder.

The young man paused momentarily then said, "No, I will catch a taxi to the Arlington National Cemetery to see my dad. Then I'll stay with my aunt a day or two. You see, my dad was killed by an enemy's IED in Iraq a few months after I was born. Like you, he sacrificed his life for our country so we can enjoy the freedom that we have and for the freedom of the people halfway around the world that he didn't even know. I never knew my dad and never had a chance to say goodbye.

But there isn't a day, as long as I'm old enough to remember, that I don't think about him. I'm very proud of my dad and grateful for what he did. He is my hero. I gave you my seat not only because I'm grateful for what you did for our nation but because I wanted to do something good to honor my dad. Thank you for allowing me the opportunity! You are our hero."

The old veteran put down his duffel bag, stood up tall, and saluted the young man then, with tears rolling down his cheeks, said, "No sir, YOU are the hero today. You renewed faith in this old man's anguished soul and love in his callused heart. In a society where many of your contemporaries looted and burned when they didn't get their way or ran to "'safe spaces'" when they felt threatened or even desecrated the American flag in the name of social justice, you, son, restore our nation's faith that good men and women can and will fight and protect this nation from depravity and decay. Happy 4th of July, son."

"Happy 4th of July, sir" the young man responded and with that, they went their separate ways.

Happy 4th of July, family and friends! I hope you're enjoying this awesome holiday. Remember freedom is not free but bought by the lives and limbs of freedom fighters! Think of them and thank them for our privilege to be Americans. God bless the USA!

"This nation will remain the land of the free only so long as it is the home of the brave."

–Elmer Davis

"With freedom comes responsibility."

– Eleanor Roosevelt

An Old Man in an Old Car
(A Christmas story)

It is a little after 5:00 PM and just about one week before Christmas. The sky is turning dark and streetlights come alive with glittering ornaments. The city looks festive and the winter air is nippy. Rush hour traffic is expectedly heavier than usual. Vehicles move slowly and impatiently in all directions. Some people are trying to get to a mall after work for holiday shopping. Some are looking for grocery stores on the way home to stock up for their planned family feasts. Some are just trying to get home. But on the Memorial Parkway, the major artery coursing through this mid-size city, traffic seems to come to a crawl. A bespectacled old man in what looks like an old Cadillac is apparently driving slowly in the fast lane and holding up traffic. His nose is almost stuck to the windshield and both hands are on top of the steering wheel as though he's in a world of his own. Temper flares and horns blare as the old man seems to be unaware of the mess he is causing. "Get over to the slow lane, old man!"" someone yells through his car window as that person passes the old Cadillac. "Hey, what the heck!"" another driver heckles as she passes. Most just stare at the old man when they go around him as if what's in their thoughts are: *"He should be off the road"* or *"Old people shouldn't be allowed to drive"*.

An hour or so later, the old man stops his car on the driveway of a modest home. He is a retired physicist. He married his high school sweetheart who is now a retired school teacher. Currently in their eighties having no children and no living relatives, all they have is each other. The medical expenses have robbed them most of their life savings, and staying in an assisted living facility is beyond their reach, even if they were able to sell their old home. As he opens the front door, a sweet voice greets him:

"I'm glad you're home, honey! I was starting to worry about you. How did the eye doctor appointment go?"

"It went OK. He had a full schedule today and was an hour behind so that's why I'm home late. He said I lost most of the vision in the left eye and there was so much scarring there that more surgery wouldn't help. The right eye has early retinal detachment and he recommends laser surgery soon."

"Oh, I'm so sorry!"

"That's OK. It's just that it's getting harder to drive at night. I have to concentrate to stay on the road and I try to drive on the far left lane when I can, so I can see people better as they pass me on the right. Oh, I did stop by the pharmacy and picked up your prescription. How is your nausea?"

"It's somewhat better. I'm able to tolerate some liquids today. The last round of chemotherapy really did a number on me. I'm sorry I wasn't able to help you drive to your eye doctor appointment today." The woman reaches out and holds her husband's hand as her eyes well up.

"You didn't need to do that, sweetheart. Not when your immune system was still down from the last treatment."

He hangs up his coat then puts his arm around her waist and she puts hers around his as they head toward the kitchen together. They walk past a Christmas tree in the living room. It is small and unfinished but it adorns the most important ornament of all, the star of Bethlehem.

"I love you, Joseph!"" she whispers.

"I love you too, Mary!"" he responds.

In the hustle and bustle of the holidays, let's be more patient with the old people on the roads. They are doing the best they can in a world that's so anxious to pass them by. We don't know the circumstances they are in to judge them so harshly. How about the unkempt lady holding up the grocery store checkout line by going through her stack of coupons to see which one is still valid? These coupons could be the difference between her family having enough to eat for dinner that night or not. How about the homeless man making us miss our turn at the traffic light since he's too slow crossing the intersection with a shopping cart? It could be that he's not in a hurry because where he goes to rest is always vacant.

It is good to celebrate the birth of our Lord and Savior by spending quality time with loved ones over sumptuous meals and gifting each other generously, next to the fireplaces and the decked out Christmas trees while Christmas carols fill the air. But let's also be patient and generous with the elderly, the infirmed and the "have nots." After all, they are near and dear to God's heart. Remember where and how the Son of God was born? This story has been told and heard so many times that we tend to overlook its significance. In the hustle and bustle of those days, the world was all too eager to bypass a peasant Jewish couple also by the names of Mary and Joseph. He was an uneducated carpenter and she was an unwed mother. I wonder how many times they were sneered at for holding up the traffic as the pregnant girl couldn't travel fast enough on a donkey. Stranded and in desperation, Mary gave birth to Jesus in an animal dwelling on one cold night. The only light that illuminated the place that night was that from the star of Bethlehem. That's how God's Son came to us. He came as the least of the least. God would be more delighted with how well we treat the least among us than how well we treat ourselves this Christmas. Let's honor God and celebrate the birth of His Son by loving one another, including our neighbors who hold up traffic on the busy streets or the lines at the crowded checkout registers. When the opportunity comes, let's "not forget to entertain strangers, for by doing so, some have entertained angels unaware." Have a Merry Christmas everyone!

Image by Igor Schubin from Pixabay

"Do not forget to entertain strangers, for by so doing, some people have entertained angels without knowing it."

– HEBREWS 13:2, NIV

The Cardinal

(An Alabama Christmas Story)

She gets up and puts on her sweater and slippers before the rooster crows. It's still pitch-black outside and the winter chill seems to have permeated through the bedroom window. It's a few days before Christmas and her two children will be coming home today from their respective colleges and she wants to welcome them home with a feast. She turns on the bedside lamp then walks to the kitchen. She wants to get a head start as it will take some time to get the dough ready for buttermilk biscuits, cornbread, and a pecan pie. The chicken needs some preparation for deep frying and the honey baked ham from the freezer also needs a few hours to thaw. And then there are the deviled eggs, the cranberry sauce, the sweet potatoes and collard greens, and of course her children's favorite: the homemade cinnamon-sprinkled egg-nog. This will be their first Christmas without their dad who recently passed away from a devastating illness. She exchanges the sweater for an apron then walks over to the adjacent living room to put more logs in the fireplace before immersing herself in the kitchen. She walks past a simple but elegant Christmas tree with a few boxes of presents that are meticulously wrapped. The scent of the fresh pines lifts her spirit and the cracking sound of the burning wood warms her heart but as the orange glow from the fireplace reveals her husband's empty leather chair nearby, her soul is gripped with sorrow. He used to sit there after dinner and enjoyed his many paperback novels. She turns on the TV, trying to drown out her emotions, then walks back to the kitchen.

As the morning awakens and the first sunlight shines through the kitchen windows, she remembers her husband's favorite thing to do every morning during the last few months of his life: sitting in his rocking chair on the back porch birdwatching with his binoculars. His favorite is the cardinals. He often said they represented vitality and undying faith. As a Christian, he also liked to mention that their deep red color symbolized the blood of Jesus that covered our sins so that we could have an eternal life with Him in heaven.

The aroma of the freshly baked goods fill the kitchen as her thought turns to her children. They must be looking forward to home cooked meals and getting away from the monotonous cafeteria cuisine and fast foods. Her daughter is in her first year as a nursing student. Her son is finishing up his MBA degree and plans to come home and help her run the farm and their family's produce business. Their dad would have been so proud of both of them and she had wished he would live long enough to at least see one of them graduate. The last thought catches her off guard and her eyes well up with tears. Overcome with emotions and feeling stymied in the kitchen, she tears off the apron and runs out to the back porch.

She composes herself as the cold winter air fills her lungs and the gentle wind caresses her face. As she looks at the field, the mist begins to dissipate and reveals bales of hay. She's reminded then that there's much work left to do in the kitchen. She turns around to go back inside when at the corner of her eye she catches, on an armrest of her late husband's rocking chair, the sight of a ... cardinal!

They look at each other intently as her tears again freely flow, but this time the teardrops are accompanied by a heartfelt smile. A few moments go by as they seem to connect to each other in spirit. She whispers "I love you too!" and from those tender words, the cardinal flies away. Her gaze follows the creature as it disappears into the Alabama winter morning. The crimson-red clouds slowly give way to the orange and blue sky. She looks up and from her heart comes gratitude and a prayer: "Thank you Jesus for this gift! Thank you for today's blessings! Please take good care of him for us! Until we see y'all in heaven, it is well with us down here and it is well with our souls this Christmas!"

Family and friends, I wish your Christmas will be merry and bright and you will be blessed with everything your hearts desire. Say a special prayer for those who lost their loved ones as their holidays will be celebrated with an empty chair or two. Just like the fire in a fireplace, the holiday season can warm the hearts of many but it can also accentuate the pain of losses of others. Remind them that their loved ones are "taken care of" by the One whose birthday we are celebrating and pray that it is well for everyone. Merry Christmas!

"Hope is the thing with feathers that perches in the soul—and sings the tunes without the words—and never stops at all."

– Emily Dickinson

"I'd rather learn from one bird how to sing than to teach ten thousand stars how not to dance."

– E.E.Cummings

Dancing With Shadow
(New Year)

Dance with me, shadow on the wall.
New Year brings the promise of a new beginning for all.
Dance with me from the midnight clear to the morning dew.
As for me, New Year is also a promise that I am one year closer to
dancing with you.
Where you are, all tears have been wiped away.
But where I am, sorrow sometimes reigns since you are so far away.
Hold me tight, shadow on the wall.
When we dance, I won't stumble and fall.
The ghost of year past has been forgotten by many.
As for me, the pain of losing you is deeper than any.
Where you are, angels rejoice in dancing with you.
But where I am, dancing with shadow is the closest thing to
dancing with you.
Dance with me, shadow on the wall.
New Year brings the promise of a new beginning for all.
Dance with me from the winter chill to the misty fall.

As for me, it's faith in God's promise for eternal reunion for us all.
Between heaven and earth is a bridge too far.
So dancing with shadow is dancing with you from afar.

This is a tribute to my family and to all who miss our loved ones in heaven. May God's love fill our hearts and His peace comfort our souls in times of sadness. May we be assured that the ones we miss in heaven are dancing with angels until the days we can again dance with them.

Whatever good taken from us is only temporary. Let us live life to the fullest and accept what's given to us with joy and gratitude. In the end, it's not sadness but joy and gratitude that will be everlasting. Happy New Year!

"So also you have sorrow now, but I will see you again,
and your hearts will rejoice, and no one will take your
joy from you."

– John 16:22, ESV

WHEN HEAVEN TOUCHES EARTH
(Easter)

When was the last time you had a glimpse of heaven? When was the last time that through the fog, you could see a piece eternity? Was it when that beautiful face smiling at you on one moonlit night? Was it the tender touch of her (or his) gentle hand? Or when you held your newborn for the first time and realized that there was much more to life than your eyes could see or your heart could hold? Was it the sight of the wayward son coming home safe and sound? Was it the moment when you gazed into your mother's eyes for the last time and, through the tears, you could see the love that would last long after she's gone? Was it the favorite worship song that inexplicably resonated within the deepest part of your being? Those were the moments that "heaven touched earth."

Where is it that your soul rejoices and your heart is full, the moment you're there? Is it at the beach where the rhythm of the sea resets your spirit, where the lapping waves wash away all worries, and where the sand on your feet erases all stress? Is it deep in the woods, down by the river or high in the mountains, that the weight of the world is lifted from your shoulder because you feel God's breath in the wind and His heartbeats in nature? For me it's in my truck, driving on lonely country roads at dawn that I can feel the presence of my Creator. Those are the places where "heaven touches earth."

We're living in a world that belongs to evil. It is C. S. Lewis (in his book *Mere Christianity*) who wrote "Enemy-occupied territory—that is what this world is." We are spiritual beings who are going through a human experience here on earth. There are certain places and times that our spirit is one with God's. Because of our forefather's sin, we have to go through life behind the enemy's line in human forms. And behind the enemy's line, unless we completely surrender to the earthly desires and their deadly snares, we will constantly be pursued by the dark force and strafed by its relentless fire. Perhaps that's why bad things happen to good people here. That's why cancer strikes someone at the fullness of his or her life or even before. That's why children are cut down by crazed gunmen at schools. That's why people are lured into human trafficking by other human beings. The enemy is hard at work behind each depravity.

But God is also hard at work in His rescue mission. He sent His own son behind the enemy's line for our salvation and to die a human death as a consequence. The battle is already won and His children, those who follow His light out of darkness, have already been rescued. But we won't come home until we cross the divide between heaven and earth. In the meantime, we must endure and withstand the enemy's relentless assaults. I used to question God why bad things happen to good people. I now stand amazed why good things even happen at all and I thank Him for every blessing. It is because of God's grace that we have moments that "heaven touches earth." It is in those moments of times and places that God allows us to have a glimpse of heaven, a promise of our eternal home. It is His way of encouraging and comforting us while we're still behind the enemy's line. Every time that we marvel at the beauty and majesty of sunrises and sunsets, we're reminded of His glory. But I suspect that in His sovereign will, it is at those moments that He also wants to remind us that He is here on earth as He is in heaven. He is here, behind the enemy's line, to tend to the wounded, to carry the fallen home, to comfort the broken-hearted, to feed the hungry, to clothe the naked, and look for the lost—all through us. And He is also in the midst of what are beautiful and what are worth fighting for on earth. He's with us as we're going through the murks and mires of life and the booby traps of sins. And when our sins abound, His grace abounds even more. And He's with us in every moment that "heaven touches earth."

Why are we still here on earth if heaven is home? Perhaps because not everyone has heard the Word of salvation and He does not wish to leave anyone behind. But while we're here, we're called not to judge but to love and care for one another. Like brothers and sisters on the same battlefield, we're to carry and tend to each other as the enemy tries to divide and conquer. We can be each other's "heaven" when earth feels like "hell."

This is Easter weekend. This is the time we celebrate the resurrection of the One God sent to rescue us. This is the time that we remember and rejoice at one fateful Sunday a long time ago that "heaven touched earth" and the Son of God returned home from the earthly grave to prepare a place across the divide so we can spend an eternity with Him some day.

Happy Easter everyone! May your Easter be filled with moments that "heaven touches earth."

"Be strong and courageous. Do not be afraid or terrified because of them, for the Lord your God goes with you: he will never leave you nor forsake you."

– DEUTERONOMY 31:6, NIV

FATHER'S DAY

Happy Father's Day to all the fathers who have gone home to be with God! The only gift we could give you today is the same gift you left for us–the love that transcends all things. Though you crossed that bridge that separates heaven and earth to be united with our Creator, the legacies you left behind still live in us. May your day today be radiant with God's love and may you be at peace with the knowledge that here on earth, all is well with our souls. All is well because we know earth is only a temporary colony until someday, we too in a blink of an eye, will travel across the vast divide to be reunited with you in our permanent home where God resides. Happy Father's Day!

"Honor your father ... which is the first commandment with a promise—so that it may go well with you
and that you may enjoy long life on earth."

- EPHESIANS 6:2–3, NIV

SEEKING YOUR FACE
(Independence Day)

You are here as I seek your face on this country road at
the dawning of this new day.
Your presence is as warm as the rising sun.
Your voice is as gentle as the summer breeze.
Your hands can be seen in your creations as they awake
from a peaceful slumber.
Your light reveals the beauty of this land as the morning mist slowly
rises atop the mountain range.
Your glory is displayed in the reflection of the early dew.
Your faithfulness is like the old barns that punctuate
this country landscape.
Your love is as constant as the river that courses through this valley.
Your steadfastness can be seen in the weary old tractors and rusty
silos that help provide a livelihood.
Your smell is the sweet smell of the green grass and the rich
soil of the land.
Your grace is evident in the simplest of things: the wooden fence, the
broken mailbox, the abandoned country store, the empty church, the

bales of hay, the skeleton of an old Chevy, and even the wild flowers
by the lonely road as there is beauty in everything that you created.
And the little flag that flies from the front porch of a country home is
symbolic of your blessing on this young nation.
May you be with us as we celebrate our Independence Day today.
May you comfort and bless the poor, the sick, the broken-hearted,
the lonely souls, the forgotten, the sojourners, the law enforcement
officers and the service men and women stateside and abroad. May
you heal and unite a divided nation. And may we remember that a
great nation can fall if it no longer seeks your face.
Paint Rock Valley, Alabama

July 4th, 2018

"The Lord bless you and keep you; the Lord make his
face shine on you and be gracious to you; the Lord
turn his face toward you and give you peace."

– NUMBERS 6:24–26, NIV

THE CHRISTMAS TREE

She finds a chair in a crowded waiting room of the cancer center after signing in and sits down. She takes a deep breath and takes off her overcoat and tries to compose herself. She has been in a hurry trying to drop her daughter off at school and race across town to make it in time for her fourth cycle of chemotherapy. The thought makes her a little queasy but the Christmas music in the background does have a calming effect, and the simple Christmas tree nearby is a reminder that the holiday season is upon her. She hopes the treatment today will finish in time so she can do a little shopping before picking her daughter up. As a single parent and a cancer patient, juggling the different responsibilities can often be a daunting task.

She turns her attention to the Christmas tree. The artificial spruce is aglow with tiny white lights. The ornaments of various colors are beautifully hung on the sloping branches. The velvet and silver bow adorns the treetop, down from which strips of ribbons gracefully flow. She can see the reflection of herself from one of the ornaments. Her clothes are baggy as if they were chosen to hide the weight gain from the fluid retention which is a side effect of chemotherapy. And at that same moment, she realizes how pale she looks without the makeup on.

From the corner of her eyes, she notices an elderly woman on the other side of the Christmas tree that seemingly stares in her direction. Feeling a bit self-conscious, she unknowingly takes off the knitted hat and scratches her bald head then quickly puts it back on.

The old woman breaks her silence: "It's the tree that really matters, not the ornaments."

The young patient: "I'm sorry?"

The old woman: "I've been here for ten years now. I've seen this Christmas tree around this time all these years. Even though some of the branches are missing and some others are balding from the loss of fur, the tree is still the best part because without it, the ornaments, the bow and the ribbons would have no meaning."

The young patient nods in acknowledgment but wonders if the old woman just wanted to have a conversation by stating the obvious.

The old woman continues: "Today may be my last visit here, as after ten years they might discharge me. I remember being in your shoes ten years ago, my dear. I did wonder how people thought I looked and if all this would really make a difference or not. I've also seen many fellow patients survived and many did not. But sitting in this waiting room on and off over the last ten years, I have seen in others the same thing I'm seeing in you today."

The young patient: "Tell me what you see."

The old woman: "The Christmas tree commemorates the birth of Christ who died for our salvation. He is the reason for the season, not the festivities around it, just like the tree is the center of the decoration and not the ornaments or the bow and ribbons. You, my dear, has a beauty that comes from within and the courage that shows just by being here. The beauty and courage that you yourself might not see but they are all but evident to those that care about you."

"Awww, thank you! May I ask what your name is?"

"Claire Faith. And yours?"

"Suzanne Hope."

"Well, they're calling for me. Merry Christmas, my dear!"

"Merry Christmas, Ms. Faith!"

The young patient takes one more look at the Christmas tree. This time, beyond the glitter and the glow, she does appreciate the beauty of the imperfection that symbolizes her plight, and most of all it symbolizes the greatest love story of all time. The reason for the season is indeed love everlasting.

"Beauty is what's worn on the inside. Courage is showing up when the heart is not in the game."

– Author

A Holly Branch
(Christmas)

He steps off the bus then walks a short distance to the town graveyard. The country roads are covered with a light coat of snow. The sky is overcast and tiny white flakes gracefully dance in the winter breeze. He passes a small bakery, then enters the cemetery gate and follows a narrow path that leads to his mother's final resting place. It's just a few days before Christmas, so many tombstones come alive with decorative wreaths or garlands. He makes this trip every year but it doesn't seem to get any easier.

He grew up in this small town until his early twenties but the place seems so unfamiliar to him now. He was a toddler when his father disappeared one day and never came back. He learned much later that Dad had beaten Mom almost nightly, coming home from the neighborhood bar, in drunken fits.

He was a good student and a star athlete as his mom worked different jobs to make sure he had everything he needed to be successful in life even as a young boy. She took him to church services regularly and she would sign him up for every youth retreat the church organized.

He enjoyed the early childhood and his fondest memory was being with Mom around Christmas. The Christmas tree was always full of ornaments. Their home was simple but always decked out during the holiday. She would bake his favorite cinnamon bread on every Christmas morning and each one of his presents from her would have a holly branch attached. He learned from her early on that the holly branches were symbolic of the reason for the season. The prickly edges of the green leaves represent the thorns that Jesus wore and the red berries represent the blood He shed for the salvation of mankind.

But life again took a wrong turn when he was a junior in high school. He started experimenting with weed and alcohol with a group of friends. One thing led to another and soon enough, hard drugs became the fixture of his daily life. By the senior year, he was suspended from school and was in and out of rehab facilities. He even stole from his mother to maintain the increasingly consuming habit. Despite the heartbreak and disappointment that Mom surely carried, he always received from her Christmas gifts taped with the holly branches every late December.

Then one day, like what his father had done many years prior, he abandoned his mother and left home for good. A few years later, he became an inmate of a state penitentiary far from home, doing time for armed robbery of a convenience store to satisfy his cravings. On one Christmas night, he received a gift that again changed his life—a visit from his mother, bringing with her a loaf of cinnamon bread in a plastic wrap and on it was attached a holly branch.

He realized then, that after all these years, and after all he had done, and after all the heartbreaks he must have caused, he was always the love of her life. He also realized then that he was a lot like the holly branch, with prickly leaves and poisonous berries. But though imperfect in many ways, he was in his mother's eyes the most precious thing she knew and her love for him was unconditional and timeless.

He rekindled the relationship with Mom and with God while in prison. Through a prison ministry named Kairos, he found redemption and stayed clean and sober. He volunteered as a prison counselor and was granted early release for good behavior. He is now employed by the state as a full time counselor for the inmates incarcerated for crimes that resulted from substance abuse and addiction, vowing that he will do whatever he can to help rehabilitate them and to help them mend their own broken relationships. As fate would have it, not long after he had a new lease on life, his mother went home to be with God.

His hand brushed away the snow that covers the slab and the headstone. It has been a few years but her name looks like it was etched in stone just yesterday. He regrets the lost time that he could have spent with her and cared for her in her later years. Overcome with grief and remorse, he puts his head on the headstone and openly sobs.

As he composes himself and wipes away the tears, the young man, now in his late twenties, reaches in his backpack and retrieves the one thing that's most symbolic of his love and appreciation for his late mother. He kisses the holly branch and places it on the tombstone.

As he walks away from the cemetery, the sky begins to clear and, from above, a ray of sunshine emerges as if a smile from heaven. He feels a familiar warmth, the one he used to feel in mom's kitchen on every Christmas morning many years ago. And as he walks past the bakery on his way back to the bus stop, his senses are filled with the aroma of freshly-made cinnamon breads. His heart cries for joy as he is reminded then and there that he is ... forgiven.

Holly is just as beautiful as it is imperfect. It represents our imperfections and God's perfect love for us. May we always appreciate every blessing we have, big or small. May our Christmas this year be filled with good tidings. May we remember our losses with the fondest of memories. And may our hearts be full from the presence of family and friends. Merry Christmas everyone!

"Christmas is a season not only of rejoicing but of reflection."
– Winston Churchill

Dancing with Angels
(New Year)

I am an alcoholic. I danced alone one night when I was in a dark alley with an empty bottle and an empty heart.

I am a drug addict. I danced alone one day in an abandoned building without a fix and with excruciating pain.

I am a prostitute. I danced alone one evening in a stranger's bedroom after the music was over and the still of the night returned.

I am bipolar. I danced alone in darkness one day when I was gripped with fear and paralyzed with sadness.

I am homeless. I danced alone one night under a city bridge and under a moonless sky when my stomach ached with hunger.

I am an inmate. I danced alone in my cell one day when my soul pained with remorse and my heart cried for forgiveness.

I am a businessman. I danced alone on Wall Street after one bad trade and after I had lost everything including the friends that I thought were "friends."

I am a divorcee. I danced alone one quiet morning in the kitchen without makeup and with a broken heart.

I am a widow(er). I danced alone one cold and dark night when emptiness was as deep as the abyss and grief could span a vast ocean.

I am a veteran. I danced alone in a crowded bar without a penny to my name and with a lot of ingratitude from the people that I fought for.

I am a cancer patient. I danced alone in my bathroom one day after chemotherapy, fighting an enemy from within and trying to preserve an image from without.

I am a single parent. I danced alone one midnight after the children had settled down and exhaustion settled in.

They come when everyone else has left. They care when the world no longer does. They are invisible except to those who need them. They show up when the music is over. When you danced alone, you danced with angels. They are God's gifts to the sick, the poor, the downtrodden, the lost, and the broken-hearted. Angels dance when nobody else will. They come to bring promise of a new future. May God bless you all who are suffering today! Keep hoping for better days; keep living; keep fighting; keep dancing with angels and don't ever give up! Happy New Year!

"For He will command His angels concerning you to guard you in all your ways."

– PSALM 91:11, NIV

"God love you simply because He has chosen to do so. He loves you when you don't feel lovely. He loves you when no one else loves you. Others may abandon you, divorce you, and ignore you, but God will love you. Always. No matter what."

– Max Lucado

LOVE

(Thanksgiving)

Love is not just a feeling from within but an action that binds one heart to another.

Love is not just an expression from the lips but a touch that connects the souls.

Love does not ask for anything in return but asks only for the opportunity to give.

Love cannot be purchased but can be freely shared.

Love is the only thing that is truly more precious than life and the only thing that connects heaven and earth.

Love is the spark in darkness that gives hope to life eternal.

Love is the greatest commandment from our Creator because it is the very essence of God.

Love is the reason that God came, and died and rose again so sinners are no longer condemned.

So love is the only sentiment necessary on this Thanksgiving holiday because it is the greatest gift endowed by God and the only gift we can give each other that in God's economy, has any true value.

"You can give without loving, but you can never love without giving."

– Robert Louis Stevenson

CHRISTMAS, THE REASON
FOR THE SEASON

My Christmas tree is beautifully decorated and proudly displayed because some two thousand years ago, another tree was planted on Golgotha. My ornaments are hung because of the ONE who was crucified for our sake, so long ago.

My Christmas gifts are carefully placed underneath this Christmas tree by the ones who love me because two thousand years ago, the GOD who created me gave mankind the greatest GIFT which was placed in an animal feed trough we call manger.

My Christmas gifts were wrapped in decorative papers, tied with colorful ribbons and finished with shiny bows because two thousand years ago, GOD entrusted a Jewish girl to deliver HIS gift and wrap it up in a peasant's cloth.

My Christmas season is filled with the scent of freshly-cut pines, the mouthwatering aroma of home cooked meals because two thousand years ago, the SON OF GOD was born amid the stench of unwashed garments and animal manure.

My Christmas eve will be joyfully celebrated with the love of my life by my side, my children coming home from afar and my relatives visiting with gifts in hands because two thousand years ago, my SAVIOR was born on a dark and quiet night, visited only by a handful of shepherds from the nearby fields.

My Christmas meal will be festive and bountiful, enjoyed by my family who will be gathering around a dinner table next to our Christmas tree and our warm fireplace because two thousand years ago, baby JESUS was born from stranded, hungry and exhausted parents in a cold, musty place fit for livestock.

Happy Birthday, Jesus! After all these years, you still are the reason for the season and always will be. Thank you for being last so we can be first and thank you for coming and living humbly so we can live abundantly. Thank you for being the gift of love and the gift of life. I pray for good health and safety for my family and friends on YOUR birthday. Merry Christmas to all and to all, a blessed holiday season!

Image by Pexels from Pixabay

"Today in the town of David a savior has been born to you; he is the Messiah, the Lord. This will be a sign to you: You will find a baby wrapped in cloths and lying in a manger."

– LUKE 2:11–12, NIV

CHRISTMAS JOY

Christmas is just around the corner. For many of us, the bright-ly-lit and beautifully decorated Christmas tree is the centerpiece of our home that welcomes the birthday of our Lord and Savior. We're busy making the finishing touches on our homes that look increasingly festive with Christmas garlands, wreaths, nutcrackers, figures and images of Santa and elves, and photos of our family from Christmas past. Stockings above the fireplace are hung and the gifts are filling out the base of the glorious Christmas tree. Our senses are filled with the sights of sweet treats of all kinds, the scents of freshly cut pines, and the aroma of home-cooked food as we celebrate the homecoming of loved ones. The nippy weather outside makes the seats by the warm fireplace inside ever more enticing, and the gathering of friends and family in our home even more welcoming. This Christmas will be celebrated by most of us with joy and love and gratitude for abundant blessings as any other Christmas in the past.

But like any other past Christmas, there will be those of us who will see it come and go with loneliness, heartbreaks, sickness, home-lessness, and hunger. And around the world, there are persecuted Christians who will celebrate this Christmas in secrecy or only in their hearts. There will also be many more who have not heard about the Savior named Jesus.

As we prepare for this holiest of days, let's pray for those who are less fortunate than we are. Let's, if possible, reach out and let them know that we care. Let's prove that the love for our fellow man/woman can be as bright as the lights on our Christmas trees. Let's all have a Merry Christmas!

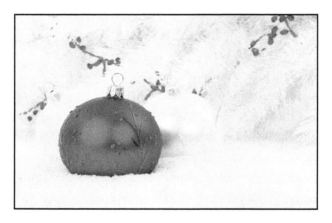

Image by PublicDomainPictures from Pixabay

"And we gonna have the hap-hap-happiest Christmas."
– Clark, *National Lampoon's Christmas Vacation*

VALENTINE'S DAY

No matter the circumstances and no matter how imperfect we see ourselves, life itself is still a gift. And among the other gifts of life, the love from family and friends is the most cherished of all. Happy valentine's Day!

"And now these three remain: faith, hope and love.But the greatest of these is love."

–1 CORINTHIANS 13:13, NIV

CHAPTER 3

THE MISSION FIELD

BANANA PEEL AND GOD

This story was told to us by Dr. Paul Sherman, a retired orthopedic surgeon from Kentucky, one night in October 2014, after we got back from a clinic in Migori, Kenya, where we worked as short-term missionaries for Kenya Relief organization. It's from a sermon he had heard from his preacher and how this story touched him deeply. I will attempt to retell this story. Though I may not get all the facts right, I hope the spirit of the story remains.

"It was sometime in the 1930s. Chile, South America, was just rocked by a massive earthquake followed by horrific aftershocks that leveled tall buildings. Many lives were lost and people were stranded without food, water, or shelters. Families were separated and some children became orphans and were forced to fend for themselves.

There was a famed reporter from the country's largest newspaper who was sent to this village, worst hit by the earthquake, to write stories on the scope of this natural disaster and human struggle in the aftermath. Let's call him Juan (because we don't remember what his real name was). Juan was raised in a wealthy Christian family. From early childhood, Juan was taught the doctrines of his family's church. He attended masses regularly and participated in countless communions all his young life. Though well versed in the church teachings, Juan never felt a personal connection with God. God seemed like a distant deity whose face was hidden behind the curtain of legalism. Through a series of tragedies in Juan's own life, God became insignificant and Juan became agnostic. Juan, however, overcame his personal struggle and became a respected journalist who had a keen eye for the human spirit and that's why he got the assignment to write stories on his fellow countrymen in the aftermath of this monster earthquake.

One morning in this village that's just leveled to rubbles by the aforementioned earthquake. Juan saw a relief truck sent by the government to bring much needed food and water to the villagers. It's a familiar scene that Juan had witnessed many times before. As soon as the truck arrived, swarms of hungry and desperate villagers would surround it, pushing and shoving to get whatever they could. It was always chaotic and every man or woman was for himself or herself. However, on this particular day, Juan saw something different. He saw a young girl on the periphery of the crowd. She was eight or nine. Unable to compete with the crowd, she patiently waited her turn. Her clothes were tattered and her face dirty but her demeanor was calm. Every so often, she would turn and look across the street and waved at four younger children who became obvious to Juan to be her younger siblings. As the afternoon approached and the crowd died down, the young girl finally got to the relief truck. Unfortunately, there was no food or water left. None, except for a banana. The girl accepted the banana from a relief worker, thanked him, then walked across the street to reunite with her siblings. Juan later wrote in his report what he saw next forever changed his life.

The little girl peeled off the banana, broke it off to four equal pieces, then lovingly handed them to her four younger siblings. After making sure they all ate, to relieve her hunger, she then slowly and carefully licked the inside of the banana peel that she held in her hands.

Juan wrote that was the first time in his life that he knew God really existed. That's the first time that he saw the face of God in the face of this little girl who demonstrated God's character, love and selfless act of service, so well.

Mother Teresa once wrote, "The face of God can be seen in the faces of the poor." Mother Teresa and Pope Francis dedicated most of their lives serving the poor because they have incredible love for them. But I suspect they also found incredible joy in seeing God's face in the faces of the poor, the sick, and the orphans.

Friends, we are not missionary or spiritual giants like Mother Teresa or Pope Francis. But please remember this: every time you volunteer at church, organize a relief effort, donate to a good cause, go on a short or long mission trip, tutor a struggling student, minister to a prison inmate, pay for somebody's meal or somebody's grocery, comfort someone who's sick, help an old lady get on a bus or cross the street, give a homeless person a few bucks, say a kind word when not asked for, or whatever random act of kindness you do to the least among us, you too, show God's face in yours. God is almighty but the most simple and beautiful truth is He lives in you!

"Truly I tell you, whatever you did for one of the least
of these brothers and sisters of mine, you did for me."

– MATTHEW 25:40, NIV

Through Gates of Splendor

Through Gates of Splendor is a best seller written by Elisabeth Elliot in 1957. It tells the story of her husband, Jim Elliot, and his fellow missionaries in Ecuador. Before leaving and trying to reach the Auca Indians of the Hauorani tribe, a fierce and previously unreached people, the missionaries purportedly sang their favorite hymn, "We Rest on Thee."

"We rest on Thee, our Shield and our Defender.

Thine is the battle, Thine shall be the praise.

When passing through the gate of pearly splendor,

Victors, we rest with Thee, through endless days."

The men never came back. They were martyred by the people they tried to evangelize to. For their faith and effort, they no doubt passed through the pearly gate of splendor and saw God on the other side and rest with Him as victors through endless days. We Christians hope to see God face to face, beyond the pearly gate someday.

But before we pass through the pearly gate of splendor, there are many gates of life that beckon us to pass through now. I am privileged to have a friend, T.C. Wong, who regularly passes through the gate of a prison to tutor young inmates math so they can complete high school education, have a second chance in life, and to share the good news of salvation with them, so they too will pass through the pearly gate when their journeys on earth end. I also know missionaries from my church, Devry and Curtis Coghlan, that for most of the year pass through the gates of an orphanage and a rural clinic in Kenya daily to care for the least of the least there and Teresa June Estes, who frequently hiked or rode to a remote mountain in Africa to pass through the gate of an untouched people and shared the gospel, and the gate of a different culture, to rescue girls from female genital mutation. I also know Brad Jenkins, another missionary from Birmingham, Alabama, who works tirelessly to cross the gates of impoverished and persecuted communities in the Dominican Republic to be their "cheerleader" and through his clean water ministry, shares with them the Living Water named Jesus and the through the solar light lanterns project, shares with them the Light of the world, also named Jesus. Closer to home, Steve and Leigh Willhelm from my church cross the gate of brokenness to provide free housing for single mothers so they can start life anew. And there is my favorite chaplain, Bessie White, who volunteers her time to pass through the gate of our cancer center weekly to minister to our patients and health care workers alike.

Most of us are not evangelical or humanitarian heavy hitters like them, but there are "gates of splendor" all around us that are awaiting someone to pass through. Local care centers, homeless shelters, soup kitchens, nursing homes, communities gripped with poverty and addiction, etc. all have these gates. Then there are the invisible gates of brokenness, depression, loneliness, and prejudice that imprison some of us. Each one of us is equipped with enough resources and skills to cross one of these gates and make a difference. It's up to us to look for it and have the heart to step across the threshold. Turn on the news and we may see people marching and protesting for their rights. But how many of those have searched to make this world a better place for others by passing through the gates of those less fortunate and really do something of substance? The scripture is clear that whatever we do for the least of God's children, we do unto Him. God, the source of all splendor, constantly looks for volunteers to send across these narrow gates. Yes, it can be costly, inconvenient, and potentially dangerous for those who choose to go, but I believe that once we seek to help those in need, our hearts and souls will be rewarded many folds because once we cross one of these gates, we'll see that the splendor ... is on the other side.

"A gift opens the way and ushers the giver into the presence of the great."

– PROVERBS 18:16, NIV

A Prayer for Missionaries

May God's light shine on your path and may your steps be steadied by His grace.

May His passion burn hot in your heart and His compassion clearly show in your hands as you heal the sick or free the oppressed or feed the hungry or clothe the naked.

May His Word be on the tip of your tongue and His love be evident in your deeds.

May His justice be at the top of your lungs as you speak for those who cannot speak.

May His comfort mend your broken hearts as you seek to mend the brokenhearteds.

May your faith be stronger than your fear as you walk through the valley of the shadow of death.

May His strength be sufficient in your weakness and His presence be your constant companion on the lonely roads.

May you seek Him as your refuge and His peace to comfort your weary soul when you feel persecuted.

May you heed his voice when He calls you home to lay on the

green pasture and be by the quiet water so tomorrow, He can again send you out to be His hands and feet.

And finally, may you not be weary of doing good, for in due season you and others you touch will reap the harvest that you sow if you don't give up.

Devry and Curtis Coghlan, missionaries, Kenya, Africa

"Let us not become weary in doing good, for at the proper time we will reap a harvest if we do not give up."

– GALATIANS 6:9, NIV

THE POKOTS

For a couple of days in September 2017 on Mt. Paka, a volcanic mountain in Kenya, we practiced bush medicine (which is a personal dream of mine) to help the Pokot tribe. The Pokots were an unreached people until Teresa June Estes, a missionary from Alabama at the time, who set foot on this mountain a few years ago, the only white person that they encountered since the days of the British colonists. Teresa brought to them the love of Jesus and later a well (with the help of American churches) which since saved countless lives. Prior to this well, some Pokot women died trying to go down the mountain to fetch dirty water (yes, Pokot women were and still are responsible for water and most everything else). This trek would take eight hours or so. Some pregnant women miscarried while making this trips. The Pokots love Teresa so much that they call her Mama Paka and gave her this mountain. These two days were special days for me and my friend TC Wong, the other white people (well, not really) since we and other Kenyan friends helped Teresa set up the first medical "clinic" there. Under the African Acacia trees, in a makeshift clinic, we did what we could to care for the sickest of the Pokots. We left the mountain at the end of the second day with heavy hearts as the needs were so great and we could only do so much. But we know God is the ultimate Physician and He will take care of His children according to His will. We loved on the Pokots and our other Kenyan friends as much as we could before we flew back to the States. We missed our families and friends at home and were looking forward to taking care of our own. God is good all the time!

"Who forgives all your sins and heals all your diseases."

– PSALM 103:3, NIV

SEEING YOUR FACE

We saw your smile in the smiles of the Pokot people running to greet us.

We felt your embrace as they came to hug us.

We heard your voice in the children's laughter as they posed for our cameras.

We felt your hospitality as we listened to their welcoming songs.

We heard your heartbeats as we listened to theirs.

We felt your pain as we saw their wounds and their broken bones.

We heard your cries as we listened to their stories.

We saw your hunger as we saw their skin and bones.

We sensed your thirst as they stood in line to receive fresh water.

We smelled your need as we were swarmed by the flies that came from their bodies as they got close to us.

We saw your poverty as we saw their simple huts.

We saw your brokenness as we walked on this barren land.

We saw your enemy as we faced the ugliness of corruption there ourselves and realized that they had endured it all their lives.

But we also saw your joy in their joy over the simplest of things.

We felt your peace as we labored in your name in one of the darkest corners of your creation.

We saw your awesomeness as we stood on the rim of the volcanic mountain where they live, the land you created.

Most of all we felt your love in the love they extended to us and the love of the people that worked with us.

Though an ocean and a culture apart and different in many ways, on these few days we were bonded as one because You created us as one.

Thank you Jesus for showing us your face as it is among the least of people and in the worst of circumstances that your face is seen and needed most!

It is here as it is in our beautiful homeland, the USA, that's recently ravaged by natural disasters, that we can endure any hardship and survive any brokenness as long as You are with us.

Whatever we accomplished or failed to, we have left it all at the foot of your cross.

We will cross any ocean and climb any mountain, as long as we can see your face.

Mt. Paka, Kenya, Africa 2017

"Seeing and adoring the presence of Jesus, especially in the lowly appearance of bread, and in the distressing disguise of the poor."

– Mother Teresa

DESERT ROSE

In the opening scene of the *Lion King*, a Walt Disney animated classic, the sun rises over the horizon of the great plain of Africa, outlining the iconic Acacia trees with umbrella tops. Animals of various species and birds of the air awake to the dawning of the new day and the sound of an African folk song to make the pilgrimage and honor the birth of the future lion king. On my previous trips to Africa, like most tourists, I looked for and admired the beauty of the exotic Acacia trees and the great migration of wildebeests and of course the African Safari's magnificent Big Five (lion, leopard, elephant, cape buffalo, and rhino). But on the trip in 2017, I was looking for something different. I wanted to see the desert rose plant and its elegant blooms. I heard about it from my friend Teresa June Estes, a full time missionary in Kenya. Teresa rescues young girls from the practice of FGM (female genital mutilation) and sex slavery. These girls grow up in extremely difficult circumstances but display such inner and outer beauty. Desert rose plants remind her so much of her "girls" that she names her work Desert Rose Ministries, in their honor. Desert rose plant (Adenium obesum) is a succulent bush that is native in certain arid areas of Madagascar, Tanzania, Kenya, and Uganda. It has a fat base and thick branches (presumably to better store water), deep green foliage, and in season, it displays one of the most elegant and beautiful blooms. Though not as big and well known as the magnificent and iconic Acacia, it certainly symbolizes something greater because it thrives in harsh environments. And one afternoon, while walking to our lodge on Lake Baringo in Western Kenya, I spotted what I was looking for: a desert rose tree.

I also met some of Teresa's girls on this trip. They indeed showed certain inner beauty despite (or perhaps because of) a very tumultuous past. Desert rose certainly symbolizes their stories well, and each of them has a story. Teresa herself, in my opinion, is a desert rose, braving a multitude of challenges and danger in her missionary life to follow God's calling.

I reflected on desert rose as I returned home and realized that I traveled 8 thousand miles halfway around the world to look for a tree that also symbolizes the people that I already know at home. My mother was a desert rose. She's an immigrant from Vietnam. Barely speaking English, she worked long hours to raise us until a massive stroke that disabled her for good. My wife is a desert rose, struggling with a chronic illness, who always puts her parents' and our children's needs before her own. My daughter is a desert rose, who's battling severe ADHD since childhood but determined to finish college education while having a successful collegiate athletic career. I see desert roses in a couple of mothers I know whose children were predators' preys. I wonder how many times they quietly wept before wiping their own tears and put on a half-smile to comfort the little ones. I know mothers who lost their children to cancers. I wonder how many times they wished they would wake up from a nightmare but the nightmare was all too real and all they could muster was some strength to carry on. I see desert roses in the single mothers of my own staff at work and in some of my patients, trying to hold their flocks together while battling their own "giants." Only they and God know how many nights they spent sleepless because of fear and loneliness. I know an unmarried nurse who adopts her grandchildren so the parents can have some time to mend and the little ones can have a decent childhood. I know another nurse who battles her diabetes, working to care for others and goes to school so some day she can educate other diabetic patients. I have no idea how many times she questioned God. All I see is how much she loves and cares for her patients. I once had a pregnant patient who was diagnosed for advanced breast cancer and declined to abort and lived just long enough to deliver her baby and another who survived a little longer to write motherly letters to her daughter. I had a young mother who delighted in making plans for her daughter's wedding as she was losing her battle to leukemia and a newlywed who faced the same illness listening to her favorite hymn "It is well with my soul" and yet another praising God while falling deathly ill. I recently witnessed mothers and grandmothers who endured harsh treatments hoping they would live long enough to see their grandchildren born or graduate. They did not make it but like desert roses, their beauty was evident to all in their unforgiven circumstances. These are just some of the many examples of the desert roses I know and I suspect you all know many more. In another Walt Disney animated classic *Mulan*, the emperor of China paid the highest compliment to the heroine by describing her as "the flower that grows in adversity is the rarest and most beautiful of them all."

I am blessed in my journey through life that I was and am surrounded by these incredible ladies. Some are still struggling with their battles and some are no longer on this earth, but in the garden of my soul, they all are evergreen. In one way or another, they help shape my own inner being. Their beauty softens my rough edges. I stand humble with admiration in their presence. It is in their struggles that their radiant beauty shines, the beauty that comes from within. Each of them has a story to tell and each is a desert rose.

Kenya, Africa, September 2017

Image by NoeliaSecret from Pixabay

"The flower that grows in adversity is the rarest and most beautiful of them all."

– The emperor in *"Mulan"*

CHURCH

I didn't go to church yesterday. I had pretty good excuses ... or so I thought. It was my birthday. I needed some extra sleep before my call duty which started at 3:00 PM. The weather wasn't the best. I could listen to the sermon on the podcast later if I wasn't too busy. Or I could just read a verse from one of several bibles I own. All I needed to do was to decide which version I was in the mood for. And if I was too lazy to walk upstairs to my study to pick out a paperback Bible, I would just sit in the kitchen to open the Bible app on my iPhone. The hardest part was probably to choose which verse of which chapter of which book that Paul wrote that was most uplifting on this gloomy winter Sunday. Forget the Old Testament and definitely there wouldn't be any Revelation. It turned out that I didn't do any of the above! I ran some errands, opened my birthday presents, stuffed myself in fried food and sweets, and took a nap. Last night, I couldn't go back to sleep after some nurse rudely woke me up by calling me about ... what I don't remember. I flipped through some photos on my iPhone to try to go back to sleep when I ran across these two photos on Facebook.

Below is the photo that my friend, Pastor John Ksinet, posted a few days earlier. The photos show a new church he's building (literally) on Mt. Paka, a remote mountainous region in Kenya. Until recently, the Pokots were the forgotten people in this African country of many tribes. There is a drought in Mt. Paka now and for some reason, malaria is rampant. I remember seeing these people standing in line to receive bags of rice or bottles of water from missionaries last September. They were hungry and thirsty. I also remember seeing them standing or sitting in line covered with flies, waiting to receive medical care from our makeshift clinic.

But on this Sunday morning, they walked a long way from their huts to attend "church." They couldn't read. They didn't own any Bible. But they were hungry for the Word. They sat on the makeshift "benches" as Pastor John Ksinet was building the church "wall" before the service. The pastor himself had paid for a ride from piki piki (motorcycle taxi) that traveled on dirt roads from his town a few hours away so that he could build this church for a people that he loves. The Pokots have nothing to offer other than a desire to hear about the God that loves them unconditionally. There is such beauty in coming as a community to worship together even if the service was in the middle of abject poverty, hunger, and sickness. Or perhaps it is in the lowest of human condition that God's love for these people and their longing to have a relationship with Him that are most evident and most precious.

Next Sunday, rain or shine, birthday or not, I'm going to haul my behind to church. Not because it is the thing to do on Sunday or that I feel guilty for missing church yesterday. It's because I want to have that hunger I once had for worship as a community with my "people." I believe our God wants to have a personal relationship with each one of us and for us to love and care for one another and worship together when we can. In the end it's not the buildings but the hearts that matter.

It is your heart, my heart, their hearts and God's heart in unison that matter. And when we come together to worship as one, whether it's here or halfway around the world, how precious it is the sight

February 12, 2018

"All creations were created to joyfully worship God.... But let's face it, sometimes worship can feel meaningless and dry.... So what can we do to increase our joy and pleasure as we worship God? One way is to recall past worship experiences that caused our hearts to soar."

– May Patterson, author and speaker

THE ROADS LESS TRAVELED

It's not the world's seven wonders but the roads less traveled.
It's not Big Ben nor Eiffel tower nor the pyramids of great pharaohs but the alleys of abject poverty.

It's not the wide gates of great palaces flanked by royal guards but the narrow doors of broken homes greeted by the smiles of the least of the least.

It's not the moonlit night on the Nile nor the romantic swaying of the gondola on the waterways of Venice but the rocking of the van on bumpy and unpaved roads to nowhere.

It's not the great castles where kings used to rule but the slumps where the King of kings still lives in the hearts of people.

It's not the sculpted or painted masterpieces, protected and preserved by skilled hands in museums but the random beauty witnessed by chance glimpses as our feet wander through the remote villages.

It's not the aroma of freshly made French bagels nor the Italian coffee from the cafes of popular tourist destinations but the noticeable stench from the places you step on.

It's not the breathtaking canyons nor the majestic peaks that will capture your hearts but the depth of poverty and height of human suffering that will.

It's not the professional hands of a masseuse at a day spa that will soften your core but the tight embrace of the little ones on the dusty fields that will.

It's not the luxurious suites of the fine resorts nor the impeccable services that you will remember but it's the air conditioners that sometimes work, the hot water that turns cold, and the creepy crawlers that might seek your companionship for the night that you will.

In the end, it's not the thousands of photographs that you take but the bond with fellow travelers and the love you have for each other, the new friends you make and the love you have for strangers you meet along the way that will forever imprint in your hearts.

In the end, in your golden years and when you no longer can travel, you will remember moments like these and smile, and from within your soul will likely come this thought: *"I have learned to live and love well. I have walked the roads less traveled—the ones that He frequently walks."*

June 2018

With Brad Jenkins of Until They Know Ministry

The Dominican Republic Mission trip June 2018

"The Great Commission is not an option to be considered; it is a command to be obeyed."

– J. Hudson Taylor

THE FULLNESS OF HIS WELL

We never knew what's in his mind but his facial expression showed a quiet desperation and an empty heart. Sitting alone on the root of a large tree in the middle of this village, the world seemed to have passed him by. Dirty and barefooted, he looked like any other kid in the community, the one they call Maggiolo, a village built near a huge trash dump somewhere in the northwest corner of the Dominican Republic. A creek or two run through this place where people wash, bathe, and drink from. Houses look like they've been built from materials scavenged from the trash. We saw liveliness and a sense of acceptance and even joy in the place wreaked with abject poverty—but not in this kid. He was invisible, seemingly frozen in place and time. His soul must have been like a well that had run dry.

One of our team members offered him a soccer ball, and right there on the dusty field of "the hole of the pigs" (which is the place's nickname), we played soccer. His world became alive. The kid became our friend and we became his. At least for a moment in time on that hot morning under the Caribbean sun, his well was full and so were ours. If that's all we accomplished on this mission trip in 2015, to fill up the "well" of a kid's soul, that would have been enough. The fullness of his well, our wells and the wells of others we may encounter was the reason why we were there. It's not through evangelism with Bible verses nor humanitarian aid with our medical bags and water filters, though we did all those, but it's through a soccer ball that we connected with this kid. In the end, when it comes to the fullness of one's well of the soul, it's not material wealth nor pious words that can fill it up but it's the human relationship built by authentic love that can—the love modeled by Jesus who called himself "Living Water."

A long time ago, Jesus met a Samaritan woman at a well, the kind of woman that even His disciples would have shunned. She was fetching water but the well of her soul must have run dry. The Son of God approached and offered her His unconditional love and acceptance. He offered her the only thing that could fill up the well of her soul—the Living Water. The rest is history. She became the first missionary that spread His Word of hope and love in her own village.

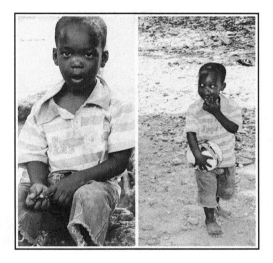

Dominican Mission Trip, July 2015, with Until They Know Ministry

"Indeed, the water I give them will become in them a
spring of water welling up to eternal life."

– JOHN 4:14, NIV

TRIPLETS!

One of the highlights of my medical mission trip to Mt. Paka, Kenya, happened today, November 2, 2018, our last day on this volcanic mountain. A mother brought in her set of triplet babies to see me for their illness. She carried two of the babies and her older daughter carried the third to our clinic. As soon as I saw them, there was in me an intense sense of awe and peace. As far as we know, they are the only set of triplets on this mountain. I looked at the mother with the deepest of admiration as she had delivered them naturally and was obviously taking good care of them. I also looked at the triplets' sister with great affection as she reminded me so much of my own daughter. Twenty-two years ago, the Lord blessed me and my wife with a set of identical triplets. Our daughter Emily who was two years older also helped care for them as I started my career in Huntsville, Alabama, as a solo practitioner. I always am grateful and feel indebted to my wife Karen for her sacrifices to carry and to care for our sons and bring them up the way they are today, and for Emily to always be a loving and protective sister.

I probably think too much into today's event. Maybe it was just a coincidence but maybe it was a "God wink." As soon as I saw the triplet patients today, I thought I heard a quiet voice whispering "you got this! You know a little more than most about triplets and their loving mom and sister." The only thing that came to me was "You always have a strange sense of humor, God! You do! But thank you!"

Then I did the best I could to care for the babies, as if they were my own. GOD IS GOOD, ALL THE TIME!

"I am as bad as the worst, but, thank God, I am as good as the best."

– Walt Whitman

A Traveler's Sentiment

No matter how far my feet may travel, home is where my heart longs to return to.

No matter how blue the sky, how majestic the mountains, and how vast the plains on the other side, home is where my soul is anchored.

No matter how exotic the beauty, how precious the people, how much work that needs to be done across the pond, home is where my mind is tethered to.

But sometimes I have to step away from home to experience the fullness of God's grace.

And sometimes I have to cross the oceans, climb the mountains, and work on His other fields to be reminded that the essence of God is love and how blessed I am.

God's love is unfettered and unconditional there as much as it is here. So when it's time to pack my bag for the roads less traveled, with humility and gladness I will heed His call. Travel I will with the sweet memories of home. Travel I will with gratitude to the ones and the One that make home the dwelling of my heart, my soul and my mind.

"Love the Lord your God with all your heart and with all your soul and with all your mind ... Love your neighbor as yourself."

– MARK 12:30–31, NIV

LOVE IS THE MISSION

Love sees no colors
Love transcends all cultures
Love connects all souls
Love binds all hearts
Love has its own language
Love is why we're here
God is love

Mt. Paka, Kenya, Africa

2018

"Love is patient, love is kind."

– 1 Corinthians 13:4, NIV

THE ECONOMY OF ONE

What do a statue of Jesus, a piece of jigsaw puzzle, a bicycle seat, and a chicken stew have in common? Nothing, really, but for a group of us from two churches in Huntsville, Alabama (Cove and Chase United Methodist), they are symbolic of why we were in the Dominican Republic a couple of weeks ago. We went to the DR as short-term missionaries under the auspice of UTK (Until They Know) ministry. The mantra of UTK is to help build biblical communities in the DR, where people would learn to use their resources to sustain themselves and not become dependent on outside assistance. The love for each other and the love of our Lord are the main ingredients that are vital to make these biblical communities work. It is about the vertical relationship with our Creator and the horizontal relationship with each other.

On the second day of our trip, we visited "Christ the Redeemer," a replica of the iconic statue of Jesus standing on Corcovado Mountain overlooking Rio de Janeiro, Brazil. In the DR, this statue overlooks the port city of Puerto Plata. There, our team prayed and prepared our hearts for the tasks awaiting us in the ensuing days. The symbolic significance of the statue of Christ with outstretched arms is self-explanatory. But for UTK missionaries, Jesus with His head facing heavenward and arms extending outward also signifies His desire for us to have a deep "vertical" relationship with Him and a "horizontal" relationship with each other. It signifies oneness as a community and the desire of the One we worship as God.

As we huddled together near Christ the Redeemer statue to prepare ourselves to be loving brothers and sisters to the poor and or sick people in Puerto Plata, Brad Jenkins, the founder of UTK ministry, compared us to a small piece of a jigsaw puzzle in the big picture that God has created in the DR. Our work was limited, our stay was short, and our impact in the lives of the Dominicans and Haitians there was small and seemingly insignificant. But God plucked us out of our busy lives to be His hands and feet and therefore, to Him, our presence there was significant for His divine purpose. We were insignificantly significant. We were there to be a small part of the biblical community He desires. It's all about oneness as a community and it's the desire of the One.

Kyle Johnson, an UTK full-time missionary at the time, told us that he had seen a bunch of Dominican kids piling up on one bicycle without a seat in a village we were about to visit. They were riding around, having the time of their lives. Our presence in the DR was like a bicycle seat. Without us, lives in these poor communities would go on without missing a beat. But if we could be like a seat to the bicycle, momentarily uplifting to them in their struggles, then we would have completed the task that God had in store for us in the DR. It's all about oneness as a community and it's the desire of the One.

On the last day of our trip, we were treated to a chicken stew called sancocho for lunch. Sancocho is a traditional Dominican "community" dish. It is often served in a large gathering where members in the community would each bring an ingredient. Some may bring vegetables, others may bring meat, and others may bring spices. Everything would be thrown in a pot and cooked together and everyone can then partake in this delicious stew. What makes it good is the combination of all the ingredients. The collective sum is greater than the individual parts. What the eater enjoys from the stew is far greater than the ingredients he or she brings. Somos Sancocho (We Are Sancocho) is the logo of UTK. We, as missionaries, hopefully contributed as a small ingredient to this stew of humanity in the DR. We hope sancocho was a little more flavorful with our presence there. It is all about oneness as a body of Christ and about the desire of the One.

Friends, if you have an inkling of a nudging to serve in local, regional, or international missions, it is because God has planted a seed in your hearts to be His hands and feet to build biblical communities. Please consider being a small piece of puzzle in His kingdom or a seat to someone's bicycle or an ingredient to Sancocho. What you get out of your involvement in "mission," as I have learned, will be greater than what you can put in it. It is about oneness as a people and it's the desire of the One. It's the economy of one.

August 2015

"Finally, all of you, have unity of mind, sympathy, brotherly love, a tender heart, and a humble mind."

– 1 PETER 3:8, NIV

This Summer

This summer I went on one mission trip and one family vacation and this is what I learned:

Mission Trip
I learned to love more deeply
I learned to give more generously
I learned to share more passionately
I learned to appreciate what I have more greatly
Family Vacation
I learned my stomach loved me more deeply
I learned my waistline expands more generously
I learned to consume certain beverages more passionately
I learned to enjoy time with my family more greatly

In my humble opinion, I needed to do both because from both, I learned to live, to love, and to appreciate more!

Summer 2015

"Keep your face to the sun and you will never see the shadows."

– Helen Keller

Blanco's Kids

O ne of the sweetest times we had during our mission trip to Puerto Plata, the Dominican Republic, in 2015 was to spend some time with the Haitian orphans at pastor Blanco's place, an orphanage/foster care home nestled on the hillside of this Caribbean nation. I have heard of the place and read about it long before this trip. Under the leadership of Brad Jenkins from the Until They Know ministry and joined with the UTK full time missionaries (Kyle, Jenny, and children), we arrived at Blaco's place after driving on a stretch of dirt road peppered with potholes and surrounded by cocoa trees. It was a serene place, tugged away off the beaten path where the orphans live in prefabricated aluminum houses donated by an oversea organization and put together with the help of the UTK ministry. We were greeted by pastor Blanco, a mixed Dominican-Haitian man in his fifties or early sixties who has a heart for the abandoned children in this area. These children are the least of the least there. Some of these children are true orphans. Some are social orphans whose parents have abandoned them or have been deported back to Haiti. The newest addition to the orphanage was a boy about five years old who was found abandoned in a horrible place. He looked malnourished and clearly suffered from vitamin deficiency and skin infection. Some of these children were rescued from prostitution or child slavery which are prevalent there.

As we entered the sanctuary/schoolroom/cafeteria, the children and the preacher were waiting for us to join them in their church service. They greeted us then sang worship songs. I seldom felt the Holy Spirit's presence as strongly as I did during the service that day. My heart was moved as I watched them sitting quietly on wooden benches listening intently to the sermon and my eyes teared up when they sang "Dieu Tout Puissant" or "How Great Thou Art" in Creole French. Jeannie Bennett Cole, one of our team members, in return led us in singing "Amazing Grace."

I can't fathom the darkness each one of those orphans was in before they were rescued. But there, at Blanco's place, they live in a small community of four or five aluminum houses surrounded by a chicken coop, a pig pen, a dried-up well, an outhouse, and an outdoor kitchen. There, boys can climb trees and pick avocados and girls can play dress up without fear of human predators. There they are cared for and protected and schooled by the loving arms of pastor Blanco and a handful of staff. There, it seems they are safe under the protective wings of the Almighty.

We left after spending some time loving on these kids, drawing and creating artworks with them or making jewelry from rubber bands and beads. Our youths probably did the best embracing them and some serenading popular tunes with them. Jenny Johnson, the full time missionary there, said it best, "When you hug the least of God's children, you hug God."

As we were heading back to our hotel, I couldn't help but realized that to these orphans, Blanco's place must be heaven on earth. From where they were in the past to where they were then, even though they still didn't have much, they at least had God on their side. In darkness, Light shines brightest and in the lowest valley, Grace can come like a crashing wave. Let us not forget our blessings and our calling to bless others, like Pastor Blanco who has done so well!

August 2015

"How precious is your unfailing love, O God! People take refuge in the shadow of your wings."

– Psalm 36:7, NIV2

Le Coco

Le Coco was undoubtedly the most simple and rustic village that we visited on our mission trip with Until They Know ministry to the Dominican Republic in June of 2016. It was a Haitian refugee village of roughly thirty homes. The place reminded us of Gilligan's island. Located just a few miles from the port city Puerto Plata, it looked like a forgotten place, isolated from the rest of the world. It nestled among the palm trees on a hill overlooking the Caribbean Sea. To get there, we had to park our van at the foothill and climbed up a steep slope. The villagers were migrant workers on farmlands nearby and most probably got here as illegal immigrants to find a new lease on life after the 2010 earthquake that devastated Haiti. Abject poverty was all but evident, but the place also revealed a simple beauty in a close-knit community without electricity or running water.

Houses the size of storage sheds with wooden walls and thatched roofs were built by the materials found on the land. Simple, impoverished, but the tranquility there was unmistakable as we stood among the rolling hills that seemed to come alive in the warmth of the afternoon sun and the quiet breeze from the Atlantic Ocean. The serenity was soon broken by the welcoming laughter of children and brilliant smiles from adults followed by greetings and hugs.

Until They Know ministry had built a small dwelling that serves as a church, school, and community center. And there, on this pleasant summer Sunday afternoon, we had "church." In the sanctity of a small place on a small island, Haitians, Dominicans, and American missionaries worshiped together. We were bound by one simple thread of humanity that was designed by God. Diverse and culturally different but for at least a moment, we were one. It was a glimpse of heaven. We brought solar light lanterns as gifts and we talked about the significance of light during the service. We also talked about another source of light—the Light of the world named Jesus—that conquers darkness and guides our paths to eternal life. Three villagers gave their lives to Jesus that afternoon.

The church site became a medical clinic a moment later. We did the best we could to ease their physical ailments. As we left, we reflected on the feeling we had that day, the feeling that Jesus' disciples must have had on their walk to Emmaus. There were many faces we saw that day. Their faces, our faces, the face of the land, and, somewhere along the way, we saw a glimpse of our Savior's.

It is often that when we walk with the poor, the sick, and the brokenhearteds that we most easily feel the presence of the One.

Friends, consider giving a little of your time to volunteer at your church, your community or wherever that your hearts are called to serve. When we lose ourselves in the service of others, we'll find ourselves in the service of God, and thus the purpose of our beings.

"Were not our hearts burning within us while he talked with us on the road and opened the Scriptures to us?"

– LUKE 24:32, NIV

A La Carte Medicine

My son Mark and I visited a community hospital in Puerto Plata, the Dominican Republic, during our mission trip with Until They Know ministry in the fall of 2013. In a dimly-lit pediatric ward, we entered a small room crowded with small metal frame hospital beds and cribs where mothers sat holding their babies. There was a single ceiling fan providing some relief in a hot afternoon. There were a few IV lines and a cast or two on tiny arms or legs of the little ones and a lot of desperate looks from mothers despite their reluctant smiles as we entered the room. All we did was to say hello and asked how old the children were, then offered prayers of healing on them. Outside the room, a lone Dominican nurse assigned to care for the whole ward was pushing a small cart with vials of antibiotics, some opened and covered with what looked like pieces of saran wrap. You see, medical care in community hospitals and doctor offices in the DR for uninsured patients (which are the majority of people here) is all a la carte. Every single needle used, every Band-Aid, every alcohol wipe, every milligram of antibiotics, every bag of saline, every X-ray are paid for a la carte before service can be rendered. I saw a mother holding her sick child patiently while waiting for a family member to bring back some cash for the next dose of antibiotic. It's not uncommon for patients to sit there for days with little care.

Oh, and the opened vials of antibiotics on the cart: they were meant for multiple patients, as nothing was wasted there. They could not afford to, as the hospital was perpetually broke. That's the reality of medical care there. It's expected and accepted.

I spoke to the nurse pushing the medicine cart a few moments later. She was a single mother, working two jobs to raise her children. Despite the personal hardship, when asked what kept her there instead of working in a private hospital with better pay, her reply was the love for her people, especially the sick little ones. As we departed, I told her that we had leftover medications—including antibiotics that we brought for the trip—that we could donate if she could use them without charging the patients for them. She cried! Sadly, hospitals around the world are more like this one than the ones we're accustomed to in our country.

God's love for them and for us is not a la carte. It is wholly and freely given. All we need to do is to accept it. We cannot repay His grace and provision and it is not required, but we certainly can try. And what better way to do that than to be of service to those who are near and dear to His heart: the poor and the sick. Each of us is endowed with a unique gift. This gift is not designed just for our own good but it's placed in us for a greater purpose. Friends, do not let your gifts stay dormant in you. At any moment in time, with your gift, you and perhaps only you can be the difference in someone's life.

So friends, whenever you can, please consider carving a piece of your precious time and spend a fraction of your resources to be the difference in that someone's life. Whether volunteering at home or abroad, what matters is using your gift to be light and salt in a world that's so in need of them.

"Let your light shine before others, that they may see
your good deeds and glorify your Father in heaven."

– MATTHEW 5:16, NIV

Maggiolo

Her name is "Felicia." At least that's what it sounded like when I asked what her name was in my horribly broken Spanish. She wanted me to hold her then carry her on my shoulder. After a few moments, she took my hand and led me to her home to see her family. She and about two dozen children were the first to come greet us the summer of 2015 when we visited Maggiolo, a village built around a trash dump of Puerto Plata, the Dominican Republic. Many villagers make a living by scavenging from the garbage. Electricity is scarce and there is no running water. But in this "hole of the pigs" which is what Maggiolo is known as, there is love and acceptance which I seldom see elsewhere. The Dominican Republic is known by many Americans as a favorite vacation destination with many luxurious resorts on pristine Caribbean island beaches. But outside the these resorts' manicured landscapes and majestic gates, there is a world of abject poverty, corruption and abuse, human trafficking that ranks among the top in the world, and racial divide that leaves many Haitian children social orphans because their parents have been deported. Despite this harsh reality, the children of Maggiolo are the most loving, the least suspicious, and the most willing to embrace strangers as guests. We were there not to change anything or to gain anything materially in return.

We were there merely to lift them up because we know that we too need to be lifted up sometimes. We were there not to bring God to them because God is already there and already working in their lives. How else do you explain unadulterated happiness in the face of hardship? We were there because to know God, we need to know the people most near and dear to His heart which are the poorest of the poor. We were there because we know that to see God, sometimes we must travel to places where God's presence is most palpable, like the place they call "the hole of the pigs"

July 2015

"But the fruit of the Spirit is love, joy, peace, forbearance, kindness, goodness, faithfulness, gentleness and self-control."

– Galatians 5:22–23 NIV

THE FACE OF POVERTY

These are the images of some children on a remote mountain of Africa (Mt. Paka) walking to or from school during our mission trip to Kenya with Desert Rose Ministries in September 2017. They were covered with dirt, walking barefooted under the sweltering heat, each carrying probably the only amount of water they could have all day and a bowl to receive whatever food given. They were not bitter. They eagerly waved at strangers passing by. Look at their faces and one may see the face of God!

Let's not squabble over things that cannot make the world a better place. Let's work together over things that can. Poverty can be seen here as it is in many places around the world.

The best sermon I heard at the time of this writing was from one of Delta airline's commercials: "The ones that likely change the world are the ones willing to step out in it."

"The ones that likely change the world are the ones willing to step out in it."

– Delta Airline

"I used to think you had to be special for God to use you, but now I know you simply need to say yes."

– Bob Goff, author, speaker, missionary

CHAPTER 4

GOD'S MASTERPIECES, THE FIELD OF GRACE

Countryside at Dawn

I like to drive through the countryside at dawn. There is something about the twilight between the remnant of the previous day and the promise of the new day that is always mystifying to me. Today is one of those days that I got up early and drove through my favorite stretch of North Alabama … the Paint Rock valley on Al 65.

This narrow country highway is surrounded by some of the most beautiful landscapes in our state, in my opinion. On this late August morning, as expected, the mist was seen gracefully hanging just above the green crops along the road. Low-lying clouds obscured the mountain range, revealing only the highest peaks. Sun light was beginning to break through in the horizon, reflecting in the glistening dew and highlighting the lush pasture below. Farmhouses, old barns, rusty tractors, and a small church dotted along the countryside. The picturesque farmland seemed to change themes every so often. Now and then, a dog or two were seen trekking by the road. Cows were spotted grazing for an early feed at every few miles. Small creeks and ponds suddenly and delightfully appeared to greet drivers after certain turns on this country road. At one point, Al 65 hugs alongside a hill as it ascends to higher elevation and there, tall trees lining the road have overarching branches that form a canopy, like a gateway that leads you to … yet another and different scenery. I did not see any people this early in the day, at least not outside their homes. The countryside was quiet and serene. There was a palpable sense of calmness and peace.

To me, on certain days, especially at dawn, driving through this country road is like leisurely strolling through an art gallery. No sooner than I finished admiring a richly colored oil painting that another one appeared. The "masterpieces" in this place are no doubt created by God and by the people who live on the land.

But I didn't drive on Al 65 just to admire God's creation and to get to my destination. I was there to be closer to Him as well. I think we all can relate to this need to be in touch with our Creator at least once in a while. In this serene place at daybreak, when nature is not fully awake, and away from the busyness and the noises of life, His presence could be more easily appreciated. The fact is He is with us at all times. We just have to fight through the fog of life to hear His voice. This morning, there was no life-changing revelation. I was just glad to be alone for a moment with my Heavenly Father and felt His peace.

It was a difficult week at work. We had to say goodbye to some of our patients and referred them on to hospice. Others grieved for the deaths of loved ones as they themselves continued to battle their own illnesses. I was looking forward to my drive at daybreak this morning. "Come to Me, all you who labor and are heavy laden, and I will give you rest. Take My yoke upon you and learn from Me, for I am gentle and lowly in heart, and you will find rest for your souls. For My yoke is easy and my burden is light" was and is His invitation.

As I drove back home, maybe … just maybe, I heard His whisper in my heart: *"I'm glad you came."*

August 2017

"Come to Me, all you who labor and are heavy laden, and I will give you rest. Take my yoke upon you and learn from Me, for I am gentle and lowly in heart, and you will find rest for your souls. For my yoke is easy and my burden is light."

– MATTHEW 11:28–30, NIV

IMPRESSIONIST MASTER

Impressionism is an art movement originated in France in the nineteenth century. It is characterized by short, visible brush strokes, causing broken lines and colors that are unmixed or crudely mixed which stands in contrast with the traditional artistic style of the day that called for perfectly blended pigments and smooth lines. The impressionists liked to paint realistic portraits and scenes of modern life which differed from the traditional, preimpressionistic artists who reveled in biblical, mythological, or historical events. One was more playful and imperfect but real, and the other more traditional and "serious" and perhaps pretentious. At its inception, the impressionists were brutally chastised by the traditional artists. Impressionism then was a derogatory term and to be called an "impressionist" was to be implied an unskilled artist or one too lazy to finish one's work before selling it. The most famous impressionists of the day were Claude Monet, Pierre-August Renoir, and Edgar Degas. As a matter of fact, the term "Impressionism" came from Monet's work "Impression, Sunrise" painted in 1873. But as crude impressionistic style may have been initially perceived, it "impressed" on or invoked in art lovers raw and real emotions and often left them with an even more appreciation for life, beauty, and love. After all, isn't it what art all about? It wasn't long before Monet, Renoir, Degas, and other impressionists were heralded as masters and were immortalized in fine art history.

But there is another Impressionistic Master who far exceeded them all. Our God is undoubtedly the most accomplished artist of all times. Have you ever stood in awe in front of majestic peaks that pierced the clouds? Or sat on the beach at dusk, gazing at the orange sun that was descending on the distant waves in the horizon? Have you driven on a country road at dawn lately and marveled at the dreamy mist above the ponds that reflected the golden rays? Have you ever seen images of Aurora Borealis on the northern sky? Did it look like God actively painting the night sky with brilliant hues using God-sized brushes to you? Have you ever had a chance to stand in the middle of Maasai Mara (an African plain) and see God's creation and His creatures as far as the eyes could see and felt completely at home? These are some of His works that invoke real and deep senses of wonder if we take the time and opportunity to see them.

But His greatest work is not always beautiful and never perfect! His masterpiece is crude and flawed and unfinished! Like the impressionistic work, His masterpiece looks, at least on the surface, "unskilled" and His masterpiece is … us! We are His impressionistic creative artwork. We bring to each other and to God the deepest "impression" of all. Imperfect as we may, the most joyful and for that matter the most painful moments in our lives have and always will come from each other! Do you remember the first time you fell in love? Or the time you held your newborn and discovered another type of love? Do you remember your toddler calling you at work because he or she missed you? Do you remember holding your parent's hand for the last time and knew that those weary eyes would soon close forever? We also invoked in God the same love that prompted Him to sacrifice His own Son for our salvation. The salvation we need because we are so flawed. Imagine the impression we left on Him for such an unbeliev-able "trade"! When it comes to us, we are not His perfect work but an "impressionistic" masterpiece, the one He desires because it's the only one that free will is allowed and the only one true love is possible. Like the impressionists in nineteenth century, France, God does not look for perfection in us. He looks for a relationship ... the one that leaves us and Him with a real and meaningful "impression" on each other. It is only through His love that His imperfect work becomes ... perfect! God is the greatest impressionistic Master of all.

"For we are God's masterpiece, created in the Messiah Jesus to perform good actions that God prepared long ago to be our way of life."

– EPHESIANS 2:10, ISV

Aurora Borealis

One of the most spectacular natural phenomena that I would love to see some day is the northern lights, also known as Aurora Borealis. Coined by Galileo in 1619, Aurora Borealis was named after the Roman goddess of the dawn Aurora and the Greek name for the northern wind Borealis. It can be seen in the night sky of northern latitudes from late fall to early spring. Its southern counterpart is known as Aurora Australis.

These brilliant and colorful "sheets" of lights have mesmerized humankind since the dawn of time. Imagine looking up to the heaven at night and see dancing swaths of light amid the stars and other celestial bodies. Imagine God using the night sky as His canvas and with each brush stroke, our world becomes alive with His artistic prowess that surpasses the works of impressionistic masters like Monet. Imagine sitting by the water one beautiful night and admire the reflection of one of the most awesome wonders from above. Watching the Aurora Borealis must be an ethereal and humbling experience.

If you ask a science geek how the northern lights are formed, the explanation may go something like this: The source of the northern lights comes from the sun. At its core, the sun's temperature can get up to 14 million degrees and fuse hydrogen and helium atoms, which subsequently form highly charged gases called solar winds that are flung into space. Once these gases approach our planet, which has its own magnetic field, they are repelled by the magnetic force and the gases have to go around the earth. But at the Arctic (north magnetic pole) and Antarctic (south magnetic pole) regions, instead of being repelled, some of the solar wind gets pulled down to the earth's upper atmosphere and this is where the highly charged particles collide with earth's atmospheric atoms. This collision emits lights of different colors depending on whether oxygen or nitrogen atoms that these particles collide with. Though only seen at night, the northern lights are present during the daytime as well.

God in His infinite grace and love for mankind constantly seeks to have a relationship with us. He gives us the freedom to walk with Him or to repel Him in our life's decisions. He is often forgotten when life is full of joy and success. But He is often sought out when life is dark and its tasks are daunting. He is there at all times. We just tend not to see Him, ironically, when "the sky is sunny" and look for His light when "the sky is dark." Like Aurora Borealis, His grace is magnificent in our darkest hour, but it's just as spectacular in daylight even if we don't see it. He is with us whether we see Him or not.

Yes, I still want to see Aurora Borealis someday. In the meantime, I am to appreciate everything else in life, big or small. Because pretty much everything in life that God puts on my path (whether I want it or not) is a gift.

Image by Skeeze from Pixabay

"Every good and perfect gift is from above, coming down from the Father of the heavenly lights, who does not change like shifting shadows."

– JAMES 1:17, NIV

This Morning

Raindrops tap-danced on my windshield as I drove through the countryside this morning. The sky was overcast with dark clouds billowing like giant guardians of the night.

Then from a distance, God dipped his brush and painted the heaven. With a splash of blue and a touch of gold, he chased away the clouds to bring forth the dawning of a new day. I had the front seat to admire the Master at work this morning as my pickup truck traveled the empty country roads.

Like an old friend awakening from sleep, the land opened and stretched as sunlight ascended behind the mountain range. And like a thin blanket from the previous night, the morning mist was slowly lifted over the fields, showing off various crops still glistening with dew. Farmhouses, crooked fences, rusty mailboxes, old red barns, lonely tractors, white churches, a country store, and a gas station or two slowly appeared like parts of a giant palette that God used for his handiwork. A small river appeared on my passenger side as I peeked through the window. He must have washed his brush here as the water was infused with the colors of heaven. A bird or two stood watching on the power line as a freight train slumbered along on its track, breaking the silence of the new day. As the morning progressed, livestock could be seen grazing behind the crooked fences and other vehicles started to come from the opposite direction. At one turn, I saw a few headstones near the road. Just like anywhere else, this land has a past and a story to tell and a future that's still untold. No matter how many times I drove through here, every morning was different and every one of God's creation was unique in its design.

Just like the countryside this morning, we're all created uniquely. We all have scars like the old barns. We are faulty like the rusty mailboxes and imperfect like the crooked fences. But we are God's best works. Like the river I saw this morning, we are infused with the colors of heaven. We have a past, a story to tell and a future that's yet to unfold. And a wonderful future it will be no matter what, because we are created by the Master.

Alabama countryside the morning of July 2018

"For we are His workmanship, created in Christ Jesus to do good works, which God prepared beforehand so we would walk in them."

– EPHESIANS 2:10, NASB

ALASKAN GLACIERS

Alaska is renowned for its majestic snowcapped mountains and cascading glaciers. Formed by compacted snowflakes over hundreds or thousands of years, the ever-changing glaciers move through the Alaskan landscape like "frozen rivers" and carve out passages that make the land as breathtaking as it is unique. From a distance, one can see the tall, sharp, and jagged upper mountain ranges that point straight up to the heavens. They seem to have been untouched since the dawn of time. As the glaciers came down from these tall peaks, they "flowed" over and through the lower terrain, acting like giant "files" to smooth out the rough edges of the lower mountains. Looking more closely, we can see the cracks and crevices as reminders that these lower mountains have been shaped by the scrapes and cuts from the passing glaciers.

But it doesn't take long for one to notice that even though the taller peaks look more majestic and ethereal, they are virtually uninhabitable. And the smaller and lower mountains that are rounded off or broken up by past glaciers? They are covered by a lush tapestry of spruces, hemlocks, and thousands of other species of plants, lichens, and mosses and are homes to countless bald eagles, ospreys, and other birds of the air. On certain "rocks," one may witness herds of sea lions or seals basking under the warm morning sun. And at a specific time of each year, salmons miraculously swim upstream from the Pacific Ocean to spawn at the exact creeks on these lower mountains where they were born, before they perish and thus completing the circle of life. And following them are the humpbacks and the orcas or the beluga whales that make the inner passage of Alaska a desirable tourist destination. And then there are the bears that rummage through the land with their cubs and the rugged people who explored this last American frontier and made it their home. Without the flowing and melting glaciers that shape the Alaskan landscape, Alaska would not be as magnificent and teeming with life as it is. Though Alaska has its own history of natural disasters like avalanches, Arctic blizzards, earthquakes, and tsunamis that have destroyed much, the glaciers will flow on to provide and to preserve lives. Sometimes beauty is seen best after the most difficult of times. After a storm, the sun seems most radiant. After a salmon dies, its offspring emerge from the pebbles below. After the Arctic blizzard ends, the heavens can display the most splendid Aurora on a dark and starless sky.

God's grace is a little bit like the Alaskan glaciers. It flows through each and every one of our lives. Sometimes our life circumstances are difficult and their consequences are cutting, painful, or even scar-forming. But perhaps because of these life-changing events, we grow and develop to better our lives and the lives of others. Sometimes we experience painful life-changing events because God loves us (and others) too much to leave us where we were. Of course we shouldn't confuse these meaningful events with the undesirable calamities like accidents, cancers, natural disasters, and other evils of the fallen world that kill and destroy. These are like the avalanches or blizzards or earthquakes or tsunamis that befall Alaska. They are inevitable as much as they are feared. But throughout the best and the worst of life, God's grace gently permeates and flows. It always has and it always will. Life on earth has a beginning and an end and through it flows the glacier of grace. And that grace will someday carry us on to eternity.

"Out of His fullness we have received grace in place of grace already given."

– JOHN 1:16, NIV

COMETS

Comets are space rocks composed of space dust, ice, and gases. There are about a trillion of them orbiting the solar system some 4.5 billion miles from the sun in the so-called "Kuiper belt". Each comet is different from the others in size, shape, and composition. They lay motionless in space but if there is a disturbance such as the force of a passing star, they may be pulled out of orbit by the gravitational pull of the sun and the journey toward the sun begins. As they get closer to the sun, the solar wind and radiation cause these "space rocks" to undergo metamorphosis. They become radiant as surface ice starts to melt and the gases within them escape, sometimes violently enough to cause these comets to crack and break up. They look more spectacular the closer they get to the sun, with a brilliant halo of gas forming the atmosphere around the nucleus and a long tail of dust and gases trailing behind. The journey toward the sun rounds off the rough edges of the comets and they become more spherical or elliptical as they settle into a new orbit around the sun. If you see a comet trekking across the night sky, the image will likely stay with you for the rest of your life. Like a chrysalis of a rock transforming into a heavenly butterfly, comets are some the most beautiful displays of God's creations. But their journey is without peril and never a straight path. Because of competing gravitational forces from other heavenly bodies, they frequently get thrown out of course and can smash onto a moon, a planet, or can simply be flung back into deep space. Most of them, however, will find their ways to a new home, orbiting the sun.

I think our Christian journey is a little bit like that of a comet. Left to our own devices, we are like space rocks floating aimlessly in the deep and dark space. By the grace of God, we're pursued, invited, and pulled toward His brilliant light. Our journey is never a straight path as we often get pulled by another competing force—the "flesh" and all of its earthly desires. The difference is even if we crash and burn, God with His undying love and limitless grace will pull us out of our craters of mistakes and chart out for us a new course toward Him. The closer we get to Him, the more impurities we're willing to release and the more transparent we look. Just like the comets, we reflect more of His brilliant light as we come closer to Him. Our rough edges are rounded off as we settle in a new orbit around Him. We are fundamentally changed as we are "reborn." We will never be perfect but God did not intend for us to be perfect. He intended for us to be loved and to love Him and one another.

Comets have no control of their paths but we do. How blessed are we who are given free will and who are forgiven even if our will frequently takes us on the wrong path!

Image by Gerd Altmann from Pixabay

"When I was born again, I received the very life of the risen Lord from Jesus Himself."

– Oswald Chambers

CHAPTER 5

HEAVEN AND EARTH, THE FIELD OF BLESSINGS

THE LITTLE THINGS

Contrary to our tendency to desire greater and "better things" in life, ultimately it's the "little things" that more likely will capture our hearts and it's the memories of these little things that will be most enduring in our souls.

Most terminal patients lying in hospital beds don't wish to come home to look at their portfolios or their fine arts collections, admire the certificates of accomplishments on their private library walls, purchase another piece of property, throw another lavish party, or plan another trip around the world. What I heard most often was about their desire to enjoy the little things one more time. It's about sinking in their favorite leather chair by the window with a good book. It's about sitting on the back porch and feeling the warm sunlight on their face. It's about dipping their toes in the pond while listening to the rustling of the gentle breeze in the nearby magnolia. It's about putting on the garden rubber gloves and sticking their hands in the dirt. It's about standing on the beach to be mesmerized by the sound of the crashing waves and watch the sun come up. It's about cuddling up with their spouse by the outdoor fire pit, wrapped up in a cozy blanket to look for the Great Dipper in the October sky. It's about sitting in a tiny fishing boat with their grandson at dawn on the lake and hoping for a good catch. It's about sharing some nachos and a cold beer with their family at their favorite stadium and watch the Tide roll or the Tigers roar one more time. And if they were fortunate, it's about surviving long enough to see their daughter in her wedding gown walking down the church aisle or their stepson graduating from the Citadel or West Point.

Most of us spend most of our lives dreaming, preparing, and working for the big things in life. And there is nothing wrong with that. But in the end, it's the little things that we long to come back to because, more often than not, they are the most memorable gifts in life. And the most memorable gifts in life all have one thing in common: the quality time we have with ourselves or with our family and friends. It is in these moments—devoid of other distractions from life—that life is most meaningful.

I'm just as guilty as anyone for chasing the big things and need to remind myself often that in the "rat race" of life, I need to slow down to enjoy the little things. So, friends, the next time you go plinking with your sons, shopping with your daughters, meeting your friend for a cup of coffee, sharing a chocolate eruption with your date, taking a stroll by yourself in the woods or by the waters, making a phone call to someone you haven't heard awhile, or doing whatever simple things that delight your hearts or comfort your souls, spend a little more time and enjoy the moments. In the end, these little things are what matter most. Until we are home with God, these little things are the stuff that make a good life … good!

"We ought not to be weary in doing little things for the love of God. For God does not regard the greatness of the work but the love with which it is performed."

– Brother Lawrence

"Little things make big things happen."

– John Wooden

Messages on the Sand

O ne of my fondest childhood memories is vacationing at the beach with my family. On a yellow sand beach of the South China sea, my siblings and I would spend countless hours catching tiny sand crabs, jumping the surf, building sandcastles, and drawing on the wet sand as our parents watched on. Years later and halfway around the world, I would delight myself by watching my own children doing the same things on the sugar-white sand beaches of the gulf coast in America.

There is something alluring about drawing on the wet sand and waiting for the incoming waves to erase the handiworks. Perhaps it signifies the carefree fun under the sun or the easiness of starting all over if the writing or drawing is less than perfect. Thanks to the rhythm of the waves, the wet sand is an ever-self-erasing canvas and beach lovers can spend an eternity creating life messages on the sand if they wish.

Over two thousand years ago, the Pharisees tested Jesus by bringing Him a woman caught in adultery and urged Him to consent her to death by stoning according to the Law of Moses. Jesus quietly knelt and wrote on the "sand" with His fingers. The message He wrote was never revealed in the scripture. Perhaps He wrote a message of repentance and forgiveness because in the end, He looked at the adulterous woman and lovingly said, "Neither do I condemn you; leave and sin no more." Perhaps He wrote down the Ten Commandments and emphasized on "Thou shall not kill." Perhaps He wrote down the sins the accusers themselves committed and implored, "Let the one without sin cast the first stone." Perhaps, as He stood up, with a swipe of His foot, Jesus erased the message of sins that He just wrote. Like the ocean wave erasing the messages on the sand, Jesus showed the lesson of grace eagerly given if one turned from the sinful way. Aside from the accused, the only One without sin that day was the only One who did not pick up a stone. Sometime later, as He was languishing on the cross, Jesus asked God to forgive His tormentors even before they repented from their wicked ways, thus again showing us His wave of mercy and grace erasing the wage of sin.

As a people, we are too quick to label each other based on our differences in skin colors, spoken languages, socioeconomic status, religious denominations, political ideology, and so on. We're are also quick to cast stones on each other if we perceive the other is in the wrong. The mainstream media, politicians, political pundits or activists, universities, and entertainment industry unfortunately share the blame for social, moral, and spiritual divisiveness and are quick to hurl insults and even promote physical violence on those who hold a contrary belief. We as a people in some ways have not evolved much since the days Jesus walked on this earth. The message Jesus gave us is so simple to understand and yet so difficult to practice: Love God and love one another.

The only permanent fixture in God's creation is His love for us, as beautifully stated in Romans 8:38. Everything else on earth is temporal and like the messages on the sand, can be easily erased. Because Jesus died and rose again, we are promised an eternal life with God, if we strive to walk in the Light. Unlike, the messages on the sand, this promise is etched in eternity.

"For I am convinced that neither death nor life, neither angels nor demons, neither the present nor the future, nor any powers, neither height nor depth, nor anything else in all creation, will be able to separate us from the love of God that is in Christ Jesus our Lord."

– ROMANS 8:38, NIV

Faith, Fear, and Love

The little boy was asked if he would be willing to donate blood for his sister who was suffering from acute leukemia. Both have a rare blood type and the hospital's blood bank unfortunately didn't have any compatible blood available nor did any other hospital nearby. Without immediate transfusion, the girl would soon die. The boy, without hesitation, agreed. As the donation procedure was about to complete, the boy grew increasingly fearful. Through tears and with a trembling voice, he asked his mother: "Will I go to heaven?""

Perplexed, his mother replied: "Yes. Why did you ask, Son?""

"How much longer do I have with you? Will I die soon?"" the boy asked.

The mother then realized that her young son thought by having his blood drained to save his sister's life, he would lose his. No matter how many times I heard this story told to our congregation by my pastor John Tanner, I was just as moved by the unconditional love the little boy had for his sister. He obviously feared for his life but had an unwavering faith in what he's willing to do.

I often hear from some preachers on radio or read from respectable Christian writers that the opposite of faith is fear, implying that fear is the absence of faith, the notion which I must respectfully reject. Fear is an innate quality that humans and animals have in common and it is necessary for our survival and therefore is designed by God. Fear is "natural." To ask someone not to fear in life-altering situations is like asking that person not to breathe when he or she is being deprived of air. What's important is not to let fear paralyze us and have faith that God will carry us through our difficult circumstances if it is in His will. If not, then there must be a greater purpose for all our sufferings. In my humble opinion, fear is not only natural: it can be endearing to God for through fear, we're more apt to pray and rely on Him and faith can shine even more brightly. Jesus feared! In the garden of Gethsemane, Jesus feared to the point of sweating blood. But it was His faith in the will of His Father that He allowed Himself to be tortured and crucified. Cancer patients feared every time the oncologists looked into their eyes before they were told what the lab work or the biopsies or the scans revealed of their cancers. But it was their faith in God's healing power and to a lesser degree—in the care of the oncology teams—that deeply touched our hearts. It is the little boy's faith that his blood will save his sister that he's willing to lay down his life despite his fear.

Faith and fear can go hand in hand and they often do. And what tends to connect them is … love. Love allows faith to shine despite fear. And love can "cast out fear" as the scripture says, albeit oftentimes only momentarily. The little boy is willing to die because he loves his sister. Cancer patients are willing to go through tortuous treatments because they love … not just loving the gift of life, but more often because they can't bear to leave the ones they love behind. Jesus died and demonstrated the greatest love of all: "Greater love has no one than this: to lay down one's life for one's friends." Friends, don't be fearful of fear because despite fear, your faith will shine and your love is even more evident.

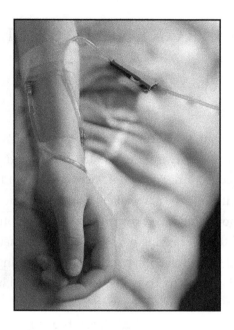

"Greater love has no one than this: to lay down one's life for one's friend."

– John 15:13, NIV

A Broken Seashell

T he seashell on the right told the one on the left, "You are damaged and broken. Nobody is going to pick you up and put you in a jar as their prized collection. You will lie here on the sand for an eternity if you're lucky. If not, a beach walker will step on you and crush you to pieces. The pounding waves overtime will finish you up and reduce you to the sand that we're lying on. What an unfortunate life you have! I am perfect and beautiful. Soon enough, a beach-loving shell collector will see me and add me to his collection where I will be admired forever. Surely, I am more favored by man than you."

The seashell on the left replied, "Even though I am imperfect and unwanted by man, I am just as loved and wanted by God. While you spend your life as a man's possession, I will spend mine as God's. As you lay motionless in a jar with other beautiful shells, I will be free with God and His creations. While your life is surrounded by the sights and sounds of human activities, mine will be embraced by those of God. At night as the tide comes in, I will be jostled and tumbled by my friends, the playful currents. I will witness the miracle of life as the sea turtle comes from the water to lay her eggs and sometime later, the tiny hatchlings awkwardly dash to the sea under a moonlit night. I will see the stars sparkling in the heaven and the reflection of the moon dancing atop the waves. The rhythmic sound of the ocean and the gentle wind of the night will be the lullaby that helps put me to sleep. When the morning comes and the tide retreats, I will be awakened by my other friends: the sand crabs coming out of their burrows, and the seabirds patrolling the beach or flying over in perfect formation. I will look for the dolphins going for the morning swim with their calves and stingrays gracefully dancing just beneath the ocean's surface. I will wave at the shrimp trawlers breaking the mist at the distance and sing along with the off-key seagulls circling above. At midday, I will be basking under the life-sustaining sun. And oh, the summer rain is my favorite! With a brief downpour, the overcast clouds will quickly give way to a brilliant blue sky with cotton-white puffs and radiant sunlight, and the rain will have cleansed and refreshed everything in God's creation including myself. And when it's time for me to go, from the stuff my body was created to which it will return, then my life cycle here will be completed. It is then that my spirit will come home to God, unblemished and whole. I am grateful for the way I was created and the life that I am given, broken and all."

A lot of us (myself included) are like this broken seashell. We should not envy those who have more or struggle less in life than we do or are better-looking or more talented or healthier than we are. God created us for His purpose and not ours so we are "perfect" in how we're formed. Look for the beauty in our perceived imperfections and our hardships and we will see the blessings. Rather than feeling envious of those who have more, we should be compassionate of those who have less. Help them in their struggles and we will likely discover the inner peace and contentment that few other things in life can give.

Like the broken shell, what's more important is how God sees us and how we see ourselves than how man does. With the right attitude, life can be ... a beach!

"My grace is sufficient for you, for my power is made perfect in weakness."

– 2 CORINTHIANS 12:9, NIV

Faith That Moves a Mountain

Hacksaw Ridge, a movie directed by Mel Gibson and starring Andrew Garfield, tells a true story about Desmond Doss, an Army medic in the Pacific theater during WWII. Like many young men in those days, Doss enlisted after Pearl Harbor to answer the call of duty and for the love of this country. But unlike others, due to his religious conviction, he refused to bear arms. He believed he could serve by caring for the wounded without killing another human being. Growing up in the South and speaking with a distinct Southern drawl and carrying less than an impressive physique, coupled with his unwillingness to carry a rifle, Doss was initially misunderstood and ridiculed and even beaten by some of his fellow recruits. He's labeled a coward by one of his superiors and threatened to be dismissed by the Army. But Doss stood his ground and prevailed by promising that he would be at the front line with his brothers in battles.

Doss' battalion was charged with the task of scaling the Hacksaw Ridge, an imposing and steep ridge on the island of Okinawa, a strategic cliff that had to be taken if the Americans were to advance closer to the mainland of Japan. Previous battalions had tried six times but failed and suffered heavy casualties. Some were all but decimated. Above the cliff, the enemy was entrenched and determined to fight to the death. Doss and his fellow infantrymen slowly climbed up the ridge. Once on top, after the initial calm, they were suddenly met with the horrors of war. Doss was not prepared for the sight and sound of hell's fury that was unleashed on them. He witnessed the bodies of his friends ripped open by the enemy's bullets or torn apart by incoming mortars. After a short advance, by day's end, the Americans were driven back and hastily retreated down from the cliff. Most were killed or wounded and left on the ridge. Doss was one of the last to leave and as he dodged enemy's relentless fire to carry one of the wounded to the edge of the ridge and while trying to figure out how to get his wounded friend and himself off the cliff, he realized that the friend had died. The next scene is probably my favorite in the whole movie. As darkness descended and parts of the sky turned blood red, Doss leaned over his friend's body, terrified, heartbroken, in shock and in tears. He then looked heavenward and muttered, "What do you want from me? What do you want from me, God?"" There was an eerie silence that followed. Then as if there was something stirring his heart and convicting his soul, Doss stood up, alone on that ridge, and said, "All right then, let's do this." He then turned and ran toward the enemy's position. God must have answered him: "I want you to try again and save as many men as you can."

What happened that night and the subsequent day was one of the most amazing accounts in American military history. Under the cover of darkness, Doss rummaged through the battlefield, behind enemy line, to look for any sign of life and rescued wounded soldiers and one by one lowered their battered bodies down the ridge by a rope so the American troops below could retrieve them. He eluded the enemy and evaded friendly fires from naval bombardment and even played dead during the day when the Japanese walked around to finish the American wounded with bayonets. He escaped sniper's fire as he zigzagged hell on earth and after each rescue he made, with hands blistered by rope burns, he asked God to give him strength for "one more." All and all, the young man from Virginia single-handedly rescued seventy-five wounded servicemen, including a couple of Japanese soldiers!

Once the news got back to camp that Doss was risking his life on the ridge to save his fellow infantrymen and even his enemies, his commanding officer led a rescue squad to help him get off the ridge.

It wasn't long before the next battalion learned of Doss's undying faith and heroism. They refused to climb the ridge without Doss being with them. My favorite line in this movie is from the commanding officer as he tried to convince Doss to accompany the troops one more time on a Sabbath day: "Most of the men don't believe the same way you do, but they believe so much in how much you believe." Doss accepted the invitation and this time, the Americans successfully overran the enemy's positions and took the ridge. For his gallantry, Doss was awarded the Medal of Honor, the only conscientious objector to receive this medal in WW II.

This is a wonderful true story on faith that can practically move a mountain (from the Japanese side to the American's). It is also an illustration on "I can do all this through Him who gives me strength."

Friends, I personally know (and I suspect you do as well) some good people who were brought to the brink of despair or unspeakable losses, but through their circumstances and faith in God, rose up and made the world a better place for many. I also know many who lost their battles from terminal cancers but fought with such grace and dignity that they live on in the hearts and minds of those who fought alongside them or cleared the paths for others to carry on the fight. Sometimes God lets darkness to befall us so we can appreciate and use the light that surrounds us for the good of others. Sometimes God allows us to be brought to the edge of a cliff to prepare us to climb a higher one. Sometimes because we're willing to climb that cliff that someone or some ones are rescued from the grip of the evil one. Sometimes we are put in the valley of the shadow of death so we can learn to walk with Him and learn to fear no evil and accomplish great tasks. Sometimes we're thrown into the pits of life so we can see that God doesn't reside just on the mountaintop but He's down here next to us to guide our paths. Perhaps in our despair, the question we should ask is not "why" but "what" as in, "What do you want from me, God?" Desmond Doss didn't know for sure why he was on the Hacksaw Ridge that faithful day until he's broken enough to ask what God wanted of him. Like his story, perhaps when God answers the question of "what" then we can see the answer to the question of "why." May I then pray for those of us who are currently in the line of fire from life that God is with us and shows us His purpose and directs our steps. May I also sincerely pray for those of us who are suffering from life-threatening illnesses that our battles can be won on earth as they will be in heaven.

Image by WikiImages from Pixabay

"I can do all this through Him who gives me strength."
– PHILIPPIANS 4:13, NIV

The Garden

There is a light drizzle and the sky is overcast on this Saturday morning as Anne drives to the countryside, something she has not done for some time. She slowly pulls up to the driveway of her mother's country home. It has been over a year since she was here, a day after her mother's death from cancer, to clean up and to discard some of Mom's personal belongings. As a single mother herself, trying to work and raise two young children, Anne had not had the energy nor resources to tend to the place so it was left at the mercy of time. She walks up to the wooden front porch that's partially damaged and mildewed, and unlocks the front door. The incoming sunlight through the windows is sufficient to reveal that not much has changed since she left the place.

In the living room, Mom's bible is still on the coffee table next to her rocking chair. On the walls are her mom's most treasured possessions: framed photos of her late husband and her children. The dining room is still intact with a simple rosewood table where Mom used to place a vase full of honeysuckle, her favorite of flowers. A widow for many years, Mom worked hard to make a living for a family of four. But she also managed to spend time tending to a small flower garden behind the house. It was her passion and beside spending time raising and loving on her children, growing flowers was Mom's way of finding solace and quiet time with God. She loved to put on a straw hat, a pair of rubber gloves, and "stuck her hands in the dirt." The garden at one time or another would be filled with the fragrance of anemone, bluebell, buttercup, carnations, daisies, foxglove, hyacinth, hydrangea, iris, lily, and of course, honeysuckle, all laid out in well-designed and manicured patterns. Mom often said honeysuckle symbolized the "love that binds" and to her it represented her undying love for her family. Anne's favorite childhood memory is playing in the garden with her siblings while Mom worked on soiling, fertilizing, watering or weeding, and her most loving memory of her mom is looking through the kitchen window and seeing her mom sitting on the wooden bench below an arbor in the garden, drinking sweet iced tea and reading a devotional book. As the children grew up, had families of their own, and moved away, Anne's mom continued to live in the house and tend to the garden. And even in her last year of life, weakened by rounds of chemotherapy, she still managed to spend some time to dig her hands in the dirt. Anne's last memory of her mother in the garden is seeing her taking off the straw hat to wipe off the sweat on her face, revealing a headscarf where her hair used to be. Anne walks on to the bedroom where she and her two younger sisters used to share. Perhaps the sweetest memory there is when as a young girl, she woke up one morning as the fever broke and saw Mom's angelic face smiling and her hair was caressed by mom's tender hands and on the bedside table was a glass of chocolate milk and a vase of honeysuckle. At the end of the house is the kitchen where Anne grew up learning Southern cooking and hearing Mom preach the love and grace of God.

She opens the back door and steps onto the garden, or what it used to be. The once beautiful flower beds are now overgrown with grass and weeds. She walks on along the gravel path, trying to salvage in her mind what once was her mom's heaven on earth. Scattered here and there are pieces of broken ceramic containers, a crushed watering tin can, a rusted shovel, a fallen birdhouse, a tattered rope swing, and other remnants of once her childhood playground but nowhere in sight is a hint of a flower. As she walks back to the house, overwhelmed by a flood of emotions, Anne sits down on the wooden bench below the arbor to compose herself. It is then that, through the tears, she sees next to the arbor … a single small bush of honeysuckle! She knows instantly that her mother's spirit is here as it always has been in her heart. She looks up and the overcast sky is now colored with a perfect rainbow, a smile from heaven.

Jesus' love is also the love that binds. It binds us to God and to each other. It also binds the wounds of loss, sickness, despair, depression, and loneliness. There are seasons in our lives that the grass is tall and the weeds are overgrown. The pieces of our lives may lay bare among the ruins but somewhere in the garden of one's heart resides the One. Like the honeysuckle, He is the love that binds but more than anything else, He is the love that's unconditional and everlasting.

"Above all, clothe yourselves with love, which binds us all together in perfect harmony."

– COLOSSIANS 3:14, NIV

THE 2017 ECLIPSE

The 2017 eclipse is over but I decided to make an eclipse of my own tonight with a Moon Pie (mainly because I'm a little hungry). But what an awesome experience it was for many of us this past Monday as we glanced at the heavens and witnessed one of God's awesome displays of majestic beauty and precision. Throughout the human existence, God has been known to use the heavens as canvas for His artistic creations, some seen on a daily basis and some witnessed only once in a while such as the eclipse last Monday. His handiwork is intended for His glory but undoubtedly it's meant to woo us into His loving arms and remind us of His grace. The eclipse also reminds us that that the absence of light is darkness, the absence of heat is coldness, the absence of love is hatred, the absence of life is death, and the absence of God is evil. For a day or so, the eclipse brought our nation together. We enjoyed the celestial spectacle and the social media seemed less replete with rhetorics on racism and other identity or political divides. To me, even more amazing than the eclipse is God's unconditional love as stated in Romans 8:38, ""Neither height nor depth, nor anything else in all creation, will be able to separate us from the love of God that is in Christ Jesus our Lord." The God that creates all things including the spectacular eclipse this Monday is the same God that resides within each one of us. Our troubles may temporarily eclipse our days but God's love will ultimately outshine any darkness. So hold your heads high, my friends. Our world is increasingly growing dark but each one of us should remain a candle that burns with His light. The One who is in us is greater than the one who is in the world!

Now if y'all would forgive me, I'm going to finish my Moon Pie (another gift from God) as I'm still hungry. I would like for my eclipse experience tonight a "totality" one. May your week be bright and filled with God's grace!

August 2017

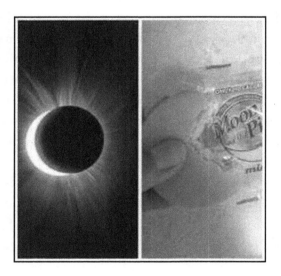

"The one who is in you is greater than the one who is in the world."

– 1 JOHN 4:4, NIV

THE CONNECTION FLIGHT

S he barely makes it to the connection flight in Atlanta on her way
to Alabama. Now living in Charleston, S.C., she has made all the
arrangements for her business to be tended to while she is away to
be with her daughter during the heart transplant at the University of
Alabama in Birmingham. Born with a congenital heart defect that
leads to end-stage cardiomyopathy, her daughter, the only child now in
her twenties, has been on the transplant waiting list for some time. Less
than a week ago, they received the phone call they had been waiting
for—the heart of a recently deceased young man had become available.

She settles in an aisle seat and as she's about to buckle the seat-
belt, she notices an older, bespectacled gentleman standing next to her,
looking at his ticket then the seat number below the overhead com-
partment. Realizing that she is in his spot, she apologizes then moves
over to the window seat.

As the plane cruises above the white clouds and blue sky declares
the glory of a beautiful day, she can't help but feel elated with the prospect of seeing her daughter receiving a new heart and a new life. She
is not a stranger to the transplant process herself, as twenty years ago,
while pregnant with this daughter, she got a call that her blood type

matched perfectly with that of a leukemic patient in Louisiana who desperately needed a bone marrow transplant. She consented and a few weeks later, after delivering her daughter, she allowed her bone marrow to be harvested. She didn't think much about it then, but she's wondering now how excited the patient and his or her family must have felt when they received the news of a matched donor. She wonder now if that patient survived and if her bone marrow had helped. It is fitting that this time, it's her daughter who will be receiving a life-giving gift.

As the plane is about to land, she turns to the fellow passenger on the aisle seat who seems so quiet the whole trip. She's not sure why, but she tries to break the ice.

"How are you doing, sir?"

"I'm okay, and you?"

"I'm great. Going to see my daughter. She's getting a new heart soon! She's having a heart transplant."

"I'm glad! Really, I am! I'm a recipient of a bone marrow transplantation years ago. I was dying from leukemia. So I know how appreciative y'all must feel."

"I hope you're having a nice trip!'" she says, smiling, as she also knows how it feels to be a donor. She's now on both sides of the aisle so to speak, having given a part of herself so someone else could live, and now she's about to see her daughter receiving a gift of life from a stranger.

The man's hands tremble as tears well up behind the spectacles, "Well, I buried my son a few days ago. He died in a car accident. He's an organ donor, so I had to stay in Lafayette a few days longer to oversee the process"

"Oh, I am so sorry! Please accept my condolence to you and your family!"

"Thank you!"

A strange thought occurs to her as she asks, "Where did you say your son was buried?"

"Lafayette, Louisiana"

Her voice trembles as she inquires, "How long ago did you receive your bone marrow transplant?"

"Twenty years ago. Two years before my son was born and when I still lived in Louisiana. My son stayed with his mother when we divorced. I now live in Birmingham, Alabama."

"I was a bone marrow donor twenty years ago to a patient in Louisiana and now I'm a mother of a recipient of a heart transplant. And you and your son…?!"

She didn't have to say anything more. She reaches over to hug the gentleman and they cry on each other's shoulder. It seems likely that the connection they have is deeper than that of mere fellow passengers on a connection flight from Atlanta.

The number of strangers we encounter over time is more than that of family and friends—some from work and some just by chance. And we may never know how deep the connection we may have with some of them. The decisions we make and the actions we take can have a profound impact on them and ultimately on us. We live in a fallen world and bad things do happen to good people. Evil thrives in killing, stealing, and destroying. But we can learn to place our trust in God's sovereign grace that all wrongs will be made right. He is just as active in healing, repairing, or replacing. His grace will ultimately be evident, perhaps while we're here on earth and if not, it will be clear in the afterlife as He has promised in Romans 8:28. It is possible that strangers often cross paths not just randomly but by God's design to accomplish His own purpose, part of which is healing or saving each other. We all are more connected in our life journeys than we think. So as the scripture implores in Galatians 6:9, "Let us not become weary in doing good, for at the proper time, we will reap a harvest if we do not give up."

"And we know that in all things, God works for the good of those who love Him, who have been called according to His purpose."

– ROMANS 8:28, NIV

Somewhere Today

Somewhere today, a butterfly will kiss the morning bloom then fly away.

Somewhere today, thunder will roar then the downpour comes.

Somewhere today, there will be two chairs on the beach but only one is occupied.

Somewhere today, a dune grass is swayed by a gentle breeze one last time then stands in silence.

Somewhere today, a loved one will take a final breath then sleeps a heavenly sleep.

May God bless those who lost loved ones today and recent days. May the peace of God comfort you today and remind you that "goodbye" on earth is "until we meet again" in heaven.

"Joy is the serious business of heaven."

– C.S. Lewis

"I would not give one moment of heaven for all the joy and riches of the world, even if it lasted for thousands and thousands of years."

– Martin Luther

His Hands

He had hands of a carpenter, callused by the tools that helped Him make a meager living for Himself and His family.

He had hands of a leader, that extended an invitation to a ragtag group of nobodies to walk with Him and forever changed the world.

He had hands of a servant, dirtied by the filth from His disciples' feet as He bowed down to wash them.

He had hands of a revolutionary, who changed mankind's attitude by His lesson of the Beatitudes.

He had hands of a miracle worker, who changed water into wine and fed the five thousand with two loaves and five fish.

He had hands of a healer, who touched the eyes of the blind and the bodies of the afflicted because nobody else would.

He had hands of a defender that picked up a stone and challenged a mob, "He who is without sin among you, let him throw the first," and saved an adulteress.

He had hands of a son, who loved and respected His Father by chasing the unscrupulous money changers from His Father's house.

He had hands of a teacher, that broke bread and raised a cup of covenant to remind us of His message of loving one another.

He had hands of a tormented, that clutched tightly against His chest in the Gethsemane garden as He begged His Father to deliver Him from impending suffering. But the same hands quickly relaxed and opened heavenward in complete obedience as He conceded … "but Your will be done."

He had hands of a blasphemer, tied behind His back as He stood accused by the same people that hailed Him king just a week prior.

He had hands of a persecuted, that were bound onto a post, as His body was shredded by the dreaded Roman "forty minus one."

He had hands of a false king, by now too trembling and weak to remove a crown of thorns that was forced down on His head.

He had hands of a condemned, splintered and cut, as He carried a wooden cross and thus the burden of our iniquities to His death.

He had hands of a criminal, pierced by iron nails and with each blow of the Roman hammer, absorbed every bit of our sins.

He had hands of a forgiver, who asked His Father "forgive them as they know not what they are doing" as He was mercilessly mocked.

He had hands of a savior, by now turning blue and numb, promised the repenting thief on the right "Today you will be with Me in Paradise."

He had hands of a loving son, whose dying wish as He was languishing on the cross, was for His best friend to care for His mother.

He had hands of an afflicted, now mottled and torn, in agony questioned God "why have You forsaken Me?"

He had hands of an obedient son, now white and cold, uttered His last words "Father, into your hands I commit My spirit" as He breathed His last.

He had hands of the resurrected, as on the first Easter Sunday, God the Father reached down and raised Him from the tomb and thus revived our hope for eternal life.

Why are we Christ followers? Because when we think of Jesus' hands, the question becomes ... how can't we be?

Thank you for Your loving hands, our Lord and Savior! Into your hands we give You ours!

"Jesus reached out his hand and touched the man. 'I am willing,' he said. 'Be clean!' And immediately the leprosy left him."

– LUKE 5:13, NIV

CHAPTER 6

THE FIELD OF TRUTH

A Morning Devotion

Thank you for the rhythm of the waves to remind me that there is order in a world that's spinning wild.

Thank you for a wall of wooden fences to remind me that courage is to stand one's ground when many are tossed by the wind.

Thank you for the random flower amongst the dunes to remind me that beauty is not what the world seeks but what comes from within.

Thank you for the roughness of the countless seashells to remind me that they come before the smooth sand.

Thank you for the sandpiper chasing the playful surf to remind me that joy often comes from the simplest of things.

Thank you for the reflection of the sun on the wet sand and the crashing waves to remind me that you are the constant amongst the variables.

Thank you for the tranquility of the sea and the stillness of the morning to remind me while others choose to yell, you prefer to whisper.

And thank you for the shade after a long stroll to remind me that you are and will always be the refuge in times of need.

Isle of Palms, S.C.

July 2018

"Come to me, all you who are weary and burdened,
and I will give you rest."

– MATTHEW 11:28, NIV

OLD RUSTY NAILS

The little farm boy is awakened by the sound of crowing roosters. Early sunlights shining through his bedroom window signal a beautiful Saturday morning. The last few days had been stormy and strong winds had caused a door of the family's barn to become mostly unhinged. He promised to help his dad to repair the barn door as soon as the inclement weather passed and today is the day. But, just like any other morning, the first thing he does before getting out of bed is to reach underneath his bed and pull out a shoe box containing his most prized possessions—a deck of baseball cards, a few old coins, a handful of painted toy soldiers, and a letter his mother wrote to him before she passed a few years ago from ovarian cancer. He admiringly looks through each item then puts them back in the shoe box and runs downstairs.

After breakfast, father and son walk over to the old barn with a toolbox and a few new wood panels in hands. The morning mist still lingers above the crops, and puddles of water from previous rainstorms reflect golden rays from above. The sky is slightly overcast with remnants of passing clouds. They clean up the shattered pieces of glass and broken pieces of timber from the barn door and pile them up with small tree branches that litter the ground. The farmer then carefully removes the rusted old nails that are now exposed from the damaged barn door with his plier and hammer and places them one by one in his shirt pocket. Perplexed by his father's action, the young boy asks: "Dad, why don't you throw them out to the trash pile with the rest, since these old rusted nails are now useless?" The farmer pauses and explains: "These nails were once placed here by your great grandfather and his friends. These nails held up this barn door for generations and helped our family keep and protect our livestock, their feeds, and farm equipment for so long. They deserve our gratitude and will be replaced respectfully."

The boy thinks deeply then asks, "How about old and useless people?""

"Of course, they deserve our love and respect as well" the farmer replies.

The boy again momentarily reflects then asks, "Is that why every Sunday after church, you go to the nursing home and hold the old and drooling lady's hands and once a week you bring food to this old drunk under the bridge and look for this homeless man that pushes a shopping cart containing his belongings around town and pray with him?."

"Yes, Son" the farmer replies. "The old drooling woman suffers from memory loss called dementia. She once was a hospital nurse. She used to stay a little longer after her shift just to sit and hold your mother's hands and comforted your mother as she was suffering and dying from cancer. Even though this old nurse no longer knows who I am, she deserves the love and attention she once unselfishly gave to her patients. The old drunk sleeping under the bridge was once a decorated Vietnam War Marine. He gave his youth to fight for freedom for a people he didn't even know and returned home to a nation that rejected and spat on him. The bottles became the only friends he knew. He deserves the gratitude from all of us even though he no longer can stand and do what his country once asked of him. And the homeless guy that aimlessly pushes the shopping cart was once a pastor of a church in the next town. He sinned against God by having an inappropriate relationship with the church secretary. He was condemned by his congregation and rejected by his family. He lost everything he had and now wanders like a lost soul. But do you know how many lives he saved for Jesus and how many unions he had presided over and how many times he had cried with the grieving families at local hospitals and funeral homes? God has already forgiven him and he just needs us to pray for him and convince him to forgive himself. You see, we should never judge people by their outward appearance but by the content of their character. Like these old rusty nails, they deserve respect for the works they've done, even now when they no longer can."

As the farmer and his son walk back to their house, the sky is now clear and the air is crisp with the fragrance of wild flowers that abundantly bloom in this Alabama countryside in springtime. Songbirds are chirping away at the nearby peach trees. The young boy turns to his father and asks, "Dad, can I keep those old rusty nails in my shoe box? I will be careful and I will take good care of them." The farmer smiles and his heart is light as he realizes that his son has learned one of the most important lessons in life. He reaches into his pocket and hands his son the old rusty nails.

"If anyone has material possessions and sees a brother or sister in need but has no pity on them, how can the love of God be in that person?"

– 1 JOHN 3:17, NIV

GARDENS OF THE SOUL

I have a number of patients whose passion is working in their vegeta-
ble gardens. It seems as though their greatest joy besides spending
times with their families is spending time working in their gardens.
And if they were able to return to their gardens after a long bout of
illness that kept them away, it was redemption! I asked some of them
why they enjoyed gardening so much. The answer was vague and yet
profound. It was because they got to get their "hands in the dirt."

Not being a gardener, I can only imagine the joy my patients have
digging their hands in the dirt and seeing the fruits (or vegetables)
of their labor. I can see waking up at the dawn of one day when the
morning light is beginning to shine over the horizon and stepping into
the garden where a season ago their hands were tilling and fertilizing
the soil, planting the seeds, watering the young plants, and weeding
while wearing their gardening gloves and their wide-brim hats. Now,
as darkness gives way and the mist is fading from the heavenly rays,
I can see the joy in their faces as they walk into their gardens one
early morning and see the lusciously red tomatoes, the plump yellow
squash, the shiny green cucumbers and various delectable vegetables
gleaming with the morning dew, and unveiling themselves after a good

night sleep. It was indeed the labor of love that created this work of art. But I suspect their joy is more than seeing their hard work coming to fruition. It is the getting their "hands in the dirt" that gave them joy and peace. It is then that they felt connected to the Creator of all things in nature.

Ages ago, God created mankind and all living creatures and placed us in the most beautiful place on earth, the Garden of Eden. Nestled between the Tigris and Euphrates rivers in modern day Iraq (at least that's where some historians think), it was heaven on earth and this was where God had wanted to have a loving relationship with us for an eternity. As we all know, due to our sin, this sacred bond was broken as it broke His heart. But God's desire was always to stay connected with us though through a great divide. It was not until He sent His only son, Jesus, to die on the cross and bridged that divide that this bond was restored. Jesus also frequently sought to stay connected to His Father by spending time in solitude in a garden. And shortly before His death, the Son of Man languished in fear and "dug his hands" in the dirt and begged for deliverance in the Gethsemane garden alone one cold and dark night. It was also there that He pledged complete obedience a moment later and offered His life for our ransom.

So I understand why some of us enjoy gardening. It is there that some of us feel at peace and most connected to God. It is the inherent desire ever since we're born. It is in our DNA. We are, as some have said, "hard wired" to long for a relationship with God. But gardening is not for all. Some of us find a sense of peace and renewal and reconnection with our Creator at the beach where the sunshine brightens our moods, the sand in our toes bring joy to our hearts, and the rhythm of the waves soothe our souls. Some prefer the mountains where heaven touches earth and there is no place more glorious, others prefer the lakes where the reflection of the setting sun on the water at dusk is one of the most magical display of God's creations, and yet others prefer spending their time of solitude at the farms fishing at the ponds. David as a shepherd must have sought communion with God at a place like such as he wrote beautifully about finding rest at "green pastures and quiet waters" in Psalm 23.

All these physical places that we seek rest and recovery in our hectic lives are also "gardens of the soul." It is there that we feel most connected to Him and see things with more clarity because our minds are not as cluttered with earthly worries or desires. God wants a constant communion with us at all times but we don't seem to hear Him as well until we step into these "gardens of the soul."

My friends, take time to find rest at the place your heart desires. It's good for you physically, emotionally and spiritually. It is also what God wants for you.

"He makes me lie down in green pastures, he leads me beside quiet waters, he refreshes my soul."

– PSALM 23, NIV

GUARDIAN OF THE SOULS

Today is the day! He was startled by the puncture of the amniotic sac and the rushing of the fluid. Not long ago, he was conceived and settled in his mother's womb. By the sixth week of gestation, his heart formed and began to beat rhythmically. His eyes and ears were clearly visible and internal organs began to take shape. His arm buds and later on, his legs quickly developed. His lungs, not yet functional, could be seen through the transparent skin. By week ten, he could make a fist with his fingers and genitals now showed his sex. By week fifteen, he could be seen sucking his thumb and a few weeks later, his mother felt his "kicks." His footprints and fingerprints were uniquely his by week twenty-two and a couple of weeks later, his nervous system was mature enough that he could feel pain. He could hear his mother's heartbeats and feel the warmth of the amniotic fluid that comforted him. Not long after that, he could hear his mother's voice. He was nourished by the nutrients coming from the umbilical cord that was the lifeline from Mom. He was protected from the elements until he's mature enough to take a breath on his own in the world that awaited his arrival.

And today is the day. He has no say on how and when he was conceived, and on this day, how and when he is brought out to the world. The emptying of the amniotic fluid flushes him down closer to the birth canal. His body was put in breech position on purpose. He could feel the cold metal forceps grabbing his legs and pulling him partially out of his mother's womb, leaving only his seemingly oversize head inside. He momentarily feels a sharp pain in his head, then with a slight movement of the operator's hands on the instrument, his world goes blank. He can no longer feel or hear his mother's heartbeats and a moment later, his own heart stops. The next step is too gruesome for this writer to fully describe but his calvarium is collapsed, allowing him to be now "delivered" through the narrow cervical canal. He was conceived nameless and on this day, he is also born nameless. His arrival in this world is not greeted by an excited father waiting to cut the umbilical cord. He won't be placed on the breasts of his mother nor embraced with welcoming arms. There won't be any tears of joy nor loving kisses on his forehead. He won't be wrapped in a warming blanket. He and pieces of him will be placed in a biomedical bag and later disposed. This is a typical process of partial-birth abortion.

Partial-birth abortion or "intact dilation and extraction" as referred to in the medical world was banned in 2003 and was signed into law by then president George W. Bush. Before that, the ban was passed by congress in 1995 and again in 1997 but both times, it was vetoed by then president Bill Clinton. The 2003 ban was immediately challenged by the Planned Parenthood Federation of America and the National Abortion Federation but was upheld by the Supreme Court with a narrow vote of 5–4. With the upcoming election cycle, partial-birth abortion ban again a topic of discussion and whoever the next president is, he or she will appoint Supreme Court justices who can uphold or potentially revoke it.

Partial-birth abortions are rare and yes, sometimes performed because the fetuses are already dead, but it's not a necessary procedure in most cases to save the mother's life because C-section would be a better option and the fetus does not have to die. Legalizing it, however, can lead to more abuses. Whether it's late or early abortion, this topic is one of the most heated ones as it frequently puts the right of a woman to decide for herself and our conscience as a society at odds. Politicians and scholars debate ad nauseam when life begins as though to justify when it's reasonable to terminate it. The decision to abort or not is always made without the consent from the fetus because it can't give us one. Who then is appointed to speak for them and this is the crux of the whole debate … is it the right of the mother to choose or the moral obligation of our society to decide?

This writing is not meant to support one position or another. This is probably the most difficult topic that I have ever written and I searched my soul long and hard before I did. I am a Christian and my faith and my conscience guide me on my position. I respect those whose position is contrary to mine. This writing merely asks how God, who gives us free will, will say and do when one of his unborn children is terminated, whether we think it's justified or not.

In Jeremiah 1:5, He said, "Before I formed you in the womb, I know you. Before you were born, I set you apart." It is clear to me what the God that I worship says when life truly begins. It's also clear that He has a purpose for these children who were or will be aborted. God, in his sovereign plan, will not let anything or anyone go wasted. Every life He created is precious to Him. Everything He created will ultimately be used to accomplish His goal, whether we, as a person or as a society, comply with it or go against it.

So when this fetus' life is terminated … the moment that his heart stops, his soul is likely taken up to heaven to be united with the God who truly created him. God is the guardian of his soul and perhaps at the moment that the fetus' body is discarded by human hands, its soul will be embraced by the loving arms of one of God's angels to begin a journey home, where he or she will live forever in God's heavenly realm.

As for the mothers who consented for the abortions, whether medically necessary or not…those that are tormented or remorseful with their decisions, God is also the guardian of their souls and longs for them to turn to Him. He's already forgiven them. He already sent His only beloved Son to our world to be "delivered" to the hands of the accusers and executioners to be "terminated" on the cross so our souls can be redeemed. God is the guardian of the souls—yours, mine, and those of the aborted fetuses! We should also be guardians of ours and each other's souls. We should guide each other, through God's Word, to do what's morally right. It is also His will that we should learn to judge less and love more.

September 2016

"Before I formed you in the womb I knew you, before you were born I set you apart."

– JEREMIAH 1:5, NIV

Your Word

Your Word was alive as I opened the Book this morning. Your Word was as beautiful as the rising mist, warm as the early sun in the horizon, gentle as the morning breeze and calming as the gentle waves touching the beach.

Your Word was as convicting as the shrieking sounds of the birds, breaking the stillness of dawn and signaling a new day of your creation.

Your Word is in the hands of the hospital nurses this morning as they care for the infirms and the hospice nurses as they caress the hands of those who will soon be with You.

Your Word is in the hearts of the men and women in blues as they put on their badges and face the uncertainty of another day.

Your Word is in the souls of service men and women as they arise this morning to preserve and protect our freedom.

Your Word is in the thoughts of teachers, as they prepare to mold the minds of young men and women so tomorrow, these pupils will set the course for the nation.

Your Word is in the hearts of clergymen as they prepare for the sermons to preach later this week, so lost souls can be saved.

Your Word is in the arms of aid workers this morning, who will embrace those facing homelessness, loneliness, brokenness and drunkenness.

Your Word is behind the windshields of truckers this morning, who travel thousands of miles and often far away from home so the rest of us can enjoy the fullness of life.

Your Word is with the farmers this morning, who through toils and worries but through faith in You help put food on our tables.

Your Word is in the fibers of missionaries all around the world this morning, as they feed, and hold and touch and love the least among us.

Your Word is in me this morning, because though I come from nothing but made into something because, and only because of your grace.

February 2017

Mt. Pleasant, SC

"For the word of the Lord is right and true; He is faithful in all He does."

– PSALM 33:4 NIV

The Greatest Love Story

Camelot is a timeless love story set in medieval England. It is also a mythical tale of bravery, chivalry, equality of the Knights of the Round Table, the quest for the Holy Grail, loyalty, betrayal and, ultimately, tragedy as a consequence of sins. After king Uther Pendragon died, his kingdom was thrown into division and chaos. His only son and heir apparent Arthur was raised in exile by the court magician Merlin. As the legend goes, young Arthur was the only one able to draw a sword from a stone anvil and established himself as the future king that ultimately united his kingdom and restored it to its former glory and more. King Arthur fell in love with and married a maiden named Guinevere, the most beautiful one in the land. Camelot which was Arthur's court enjoyed a period of legendary splendor and majesty. But Queen Guinevere was caught in an adulterous relationship with Sir Lancelot, the king's most handsome and noble knight. The queen was seized and condemned to death by burning at stake as Lancelot escaped. King Arthur was heartbroken and distraught at his queen's sentence but unable to save her because the royal decree (his decree) was death for any sin committed against the king. He could not violate his own law because in doing so, he would no longer be king.

As the fire raged and about to consume her body, Guinevere was rescued by the daring Sir Lancelot. With more betrayal and misdeeds, ultimately everyone suffered the consequences of their actions either through the pain of remorse or death itself. The once magical Camelot evaporated like the mist of an early dawn.

There is another love story that's also a story of bravery, chivalry, loyalty, betrayal but in this story, there is redemption through the blood of the King of all kings. In the book *Windows of the Soul: Experiencing God in New Ways*", author Ken Gire wrote that though growing up in the Christian faith, he did not really grasp the reason why God sent His only beloved son to die for our salvation until the author watched Camelot, the movie. Like Guinevere, the queen of Camelot, we are deeply loved by our King. Also like Guinevere, we and generations before us tend to fall to the temptation of earthly desires and turn away from God. God's royal decree is also clear: "The wage of sin is death." So for our betrayal, we ought to be condemned to be "burned at stake." And like King Arthur to Guinevere, God wanted to forgive and exonerate us from our sins but he couldn't. The death sentence had to be carried out. He is perfect and His law is perfect and unchangeable. To forgive us outright is to violate His perfect law and by doing so, He would no longer be God. He did not want us to perish nor to be "rescued" by the Prince of Darkness and live a life of eternal condemnation. Salvation had to come with a great price and through an only one acceptable and unthinkable act and that's exactly what happened. Unlike King Arthur who was frozen with grief and powerless by his decree, God took on the human form and offered Himself to be our substitute and condemned for our wicked ways. Through His suffering and death, the debt of our sins was paid in full. "Greater love has no one than this: to lay down one's life for one's friends" is what the scripture exalts and what God exemplified.

By the mystical power of his sword, the Excalibur, King Arthur was able to restore a nation to its greatness and found love, but only temporarily. By carrying a wooden cross and dying on it, God was able to restore and redeem mankind to be with Him in His "Camelot" for an eternity and thus His story, our story, is the greatest love story of all time.

"Greater love has no one than this: to lay down one's life for one's friends."

– John 15:13, NIV

DAMAGED WOOD

It was quickly cut from a dead olive tree, the kind that's abundant in the land, and crudely fashioned into a wooden post and a crossbar. Its purpose was not for noble intent like the cedar of Lebanon that formed the gate of the king's palace or the precious cypress that shaped the throne of the Roman emperor or the mighty pine that made up the hull of the governor's galleon. Its whole existence was to help condemn a man to death and that day was the day. In a place called Golgotha, the post was planted deep into the barren and rocky soil and the crossbar was carried by the condemned from the town center so the mob could have a chance to mock, hurl insults, and make the event a spectacle.

The wood was soft enough to absorb the nails that were driven through the hands but strong enough to support his weight as his naked body was stretched and hung from atop to conform to the cross. That day was the day. As the condemned's battered body sweated and bled, the wooden cross could hear the man's trembling voice questioning God's will but then begging for forgiveness, not on his behalf but on that of his accusers and executioners. And as darkness descended and the wind howled and the earth shook, the man gave up his spirit and breathed his last. On that day, the splintered and rotting piece of wood that's not worthy for noble purposes was good enough to hold the body of the Son of God as He died for humanity. On that day, God chose this lowly piece of wood to be His Son's cross. On that day, the wood was stained with the blood of the holy Lamb. Not made for noble intent but on that day, this wooden cross intimately witnessed the most amazing character of God on display: "Christ died for us while we were still sinners."

Like the splintered and rotting wood, we often see ourselves as being damaged or unworthy when we fail or life hands us devastating blows. But God sees us as His chosen and His unfinished works. The blood of Jesus covers our imperfections and washes away our impurities. And those of us who are lonely, broken, injured, infirmed, falsely accused or condemned are likely those He longs to be close to the most. He is also known to leave the ninety-nine to look for the one who's lost because that is His nature. The one who suffers most or loses one's way is the one He stretches out His arms the widest for. So we should come to Jesus those of us who are burdened and weary and He will carry us as He did the cross a long time ago. In the hands of the Master, a masterpiece can be sculpted out of damaged wood. And like the cross, true nobility comes not from human design but from allowing God's will to be done.

"But many who are first will be last, and the last first."
– MATTHEW 19:30, ESV

IMPERFECTIONS

It is in darkness that an ember glows brightly.
It is from brokenness that beauty is often revealed.
It is through the cracks that light shines most radiantly.
It is because of losses that gains are much more appreciated.
It is in the face of hatred that love is even more precious.
It is from our scars that our character is strengthened.
It is when life is hard that its tenderness is more desirable.
It is when sin is deep that grace seems deeper.
It is often in the worst of circumstances that faith of a mustard seed can move the proverbial mountain.
We should not be ashamed of our imperfections and our shortcomings. We can be at our best because of them!

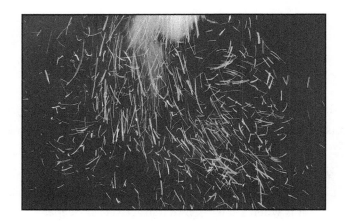

Image by fsHH from Pixabay

"Imperfection is perfection."

– Flume

The Justice for Injustice

The chief priests and the elders convinced the multitudes to choose Barabbas, a convicted criminal, over Jesus, the Son of God because He was a threat to the religious hierarchy of the day. "Let Him be crucified!" was the rallying cry from the mass. Pontius Pilate, the Roman governor, retorted, "Why? What evil has he done?"" There was no reasoning from the crowd as the demand "crucify him" grew louder. Unable to convince the Jews and fearing a revolt, Pilate (the law of the land at the time) literally and figuratively washed his hands but set Barabbas free and turned Jesus over to be scourged then crucified. This event was an injustice of biblical proportion. But God, in His sovereign will and wisdom, allowed it to happen, even at the cost of His Son's suffering and death, so mankind can be salvaged from our depravity. What man meant for harm He meant for good. Joseph was betrayed and left for dead by his brothers. But years later, through his ordeal, Joseph became Pharaoh's most trusted servant and was able to save both Egypt and his family from famine. In the end, he forgave his brothers and revealed to them one of life's most sacred truths: "You intended to harm me but God intended it for good to accomplish what is now being done, the saving of many lives." This is the justice for injustice! In man's court, there is no guarantee of justice. But in the highest court of all, all wrongs will be made right.

Until the new heaven and earth come, injustice will continue. It happens every day around the world and it happens here, supposedly the greatest country on earth. There are too many examples of injustice from our legal system that's supposed to uphold the law of the land in recent years. Are the judges and juries giving in to the pressure of a rigid ideology or political correctness? Granted that our legal system is one of the best, it is far from perfect.

Let's pray for the innocent victims and their families, especially those whom our legal system has betrayed. Let's stand by those who are powerless and mistreated or oppressed. But let us be reassured that ultimately, there will be justice for injustice from the highest Judge of all.

Image by Jeff Jacobs from Pixabay

"You intended to harm me, but God intended it for good to accomplish what is now being done, the saving of many lives."

– GENESIS 50:20, NIV

LAMBORGHINI VERSUS
OLD CHEVY

New Lamborghini: I am an Italian masterpiece. I boast a sleek design and command an impressive horsepower. Only the rich and powerful can afford to be at my control. I am the embodiment of modern design and prestige.

Old Chevy pickup truck: I was an American workhorse. I look simple but I once had enough prowess to be a part of the workforce of the greatest nation on earth. Farmers and blue-collar workers depended on me for their livelihood.

Lambo: I can go from 0 to 60 in seconds. I can reach my destination in the blink of an eye. I can effortlessly pass other vehicles on the freeways if I want to. I am unmatched in power and beauty. I am adored by the elites and envied by many.

Old Chevy: I was fast enough in my heydays. I'm now leaking oil badly and frequently needing water to keep from being overheated. I shudder and sputter when I need to keep up with others on the freeway. But I was and am always in the hearts of the American working men and women.

Lambo: I turn heads on the streets of Beverly Hills, the boulevards of South Beach, the racing tracks of the French Riviera, the mountainous treks of the Italian Alps, and the windswept roads of Dubai amid the high rises.

Old Chevy: Though there are not that many of us left, we still can be seen from the sierras of California, the desert of Arizona, the plains of Montana, to the inner cities of New Jersey, and on the dirt roads of rural Alabama.

Lambo: Millionaires and sheiks prefer me to take their girlfriends to their lavish parties. They make out in my backseat while indulging in champagne and caviar. Movie stars and their dates show me off at film festivals or award ceremonies.

Old Chevy: I took expecting mothers to their maternal checkups and senior citizens to their doctor appointments. I frequently carried livestock in my truck bed to various farms or produce to the markets. Young couples have been seen sitting on my hood gazing at the stars and dreaming about their future under the moonlit sky.

Lambo: I'm on the cover of popular magazines and featured in many blockbusters. I'm leaving quite an impression in the automotive industry and I represent a marvelous feat in technology and engineering.

Old Chevy: My legacy is found in the common people. Generation of fathers and sons have worked together under my hood and talked about manhood and responsibilities. Generations of mothers and daughters have discussed their love and devotion to their families while driving me to their weddings or baby showers.

Lambo: I am sheltered and protected. I am washed and buffed regularly to display my outward beauty. I'm kept out of the snow and rains to prevent rust and damage.

Old Chevy: I'm often left out in the elements. The morning dew refreshes my soul and the rising sun reveals the beauty of God's creation above the clouds and in the fields. When the evening comes, I have full view of the heavenly lights dancing to the songs of the night creatures.

Lambo: I'm a companion of a privileged few. I don't mingle with the common folks. I'm locked up in climate-controlled garages if I'm not driven on the roads. It's all about me and I was created as their status symbol and I would not trade my place with you or any others.

Old Chevy: I've pulled other cars out from the mud and stopped to help stranded travelers more times than I can remember. Through our encounters, I have helped some and befriended many. It's never about me. It's all about service and relationships. I was created to serve and I, too, would never trade my place with anything else.

Not all of us are meant to be celebrities or born into nobility or a privileged life. But all of us are created for God's purpose. We're most productive, appreciated, and happy when we know our purposes and stay on our courses no matter how hard the journeys may be. May our life journeys be fruitful and our legacies be what our children and grandchildren will be proud of and our homecoming be greeted with "Well done!" by our Creator.

"Well done, good and faithful servant!... Come and share your master's happiness!"

– Matthew 25:23, NIV

THE LAST FALL

O ne of my most joyous moments in life was, as a young father, coaching my infant daughter and later on my sons to walk. There they were, in their diapers and with tiny feet and wobbly legs, rushing toward me with their outstretched, chubby arms. They would fall and cry in frustration at first. Then with some grinning and nudging at my end, they would get up and try again. Or if they didn't, I would lift them up on their feet and again the "walk" would continue. As the distance closed, the awkward steps would speed up and finally they would fall into my arms, drooling and laughing or crying with joy. I don't believe I experienced any other emotion more pleasurable or loving than moments like those. The softness of their skin, the tightness of their clutches, the smell of their innocence held my heart captive and I remember wishing time could stop so I could cherish the moments forever.

This morning, while pondering the Word with my Christian brothers (who meet every Friday at the crack of dawn), I realized that our walks of faith are like those of our infant children. Like babes learning the steps, we initially would often fall and sometimes wallow in our failures. But with the nudging of the Holy Spirit and the amazing grace of our loving God, we learn to get up and the journey continues. We hope, as we get closer to Him, the falls lessen and our last fall would be the fall into His loving arms. I can only imagine the joy in His heart and time will stop for an eternity when we're finally home.

Time did stop for seventeen innocent lives at a high school shooting in Parkland, Florida, recently. Most victims were fourteen-year-old students whose lives ended abruptly at the hands of a crazed gunman. I cannot fathom the pain of the loved ones left behind. Let's first pray for them and the wounded victims. The root of the tragedy is evil and the problem is multifaceted and will require a multifaceted approach with the concerted effort from all of us. Let's then pray for guidance then work together to find a solution or solutions to better protect our children. Let's also not be blinded by our stances and insult or label each other before we even try to work together. We're all imperfect people trying to overcome a complexed challenge. We can also find solace in the belief that this week, as the stated seventeen victims and an unknown number of children dying from accidents, cancer, and other illnesses fall from this temporal realm of existence, they fall into the loving arms of God where life is eternal. On the other side, their last fall on earth is their first step in eternity with God in heaven.

February 2018

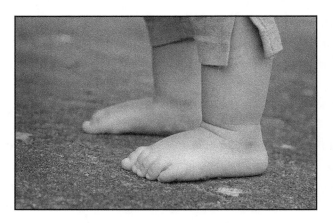

Image by Esi Grunhagen from Pixabay

"The Lord will lay bare his holy arm in the sights of all the nations, and all the ends of the earth will see the salvation of our God."

– ISAIAH 52:10, NIV

The Bassinet and the Bed

W e were placed by the loving arms of our parents in our bassinets soon after we took our first breath on earth. At some point, we'll be lifted up from the pillows of our deathbeds by the loving arms of our heavenly Father as we take our last breath here and begin our journey with Him in eternity.

In the end, what we will be remembered most between the bassinets and the beds is likely not how much we received but how much we gave. It is not how easily we succeeded but how hard we tried. It is not how much we're loved but how much we loved. It is not how many hearts we conquered but how many times our hearts were captured by poverty, suffering or injustice, and did something about it. It is not just how many times we sat on the church pews but how many times we were the church. It is not how many praises and accolades we collected but how many encouraging words we gave. It is not how many friends we had but how good a friend we were to someone. It is not how far we traveled or what world wonders we saw but how impactful our travels were and how many lives we touched on our journeys. It is not how many castles we visited where kings and queens used to live but how many broken places we set foot in where the King of kings still lives. It is not how high our position in society was but how low we're willing to bend to serve others less fortunate than we were. In the end, for all of us, it is probably not our body of works that pleased God's heart most but it's our hearts in our works that did. What matters to Him and to humanity most is how well we lived for others and not just how well we lived for ourselves, between the bassinets and the beds.

How do we know this? It's because years ago, there was a great Man who walked this earth as a carpenter's son. He lived His life humbly but because He gave, served, loved, forgave, taught, and sacrificed that we now can have a personal relationship with God. He was and is God's beloved son! His legacy on earth was built between the manger and the cross and serves as a template for our legacies which are being built between the bassinets and the beds.

"But God demonstrates His own love for us in this: while we were still sinners, Christ died for us."

– ROMANS 5:8, NIV

FOOTPRINTS IN THE SAND

Most of us enjoy walking on the beach. There is something alluring about the sound of the ocean that reminds us of the rhythm of life, the inviting calls of the seagulls from above that lift out spirit, the wet sand below our feet that relieves all stress, the salty air that cleanses the soul, the gentle breeze that softens the heart, and the sand crabs and the seashells that remind us that we are merely a part of God's vast creation. I'm always mesmerized by the footprints we leave in the sand. On the wet sand near the ocean, these shallow footprints will be quickly erased by the coming waves. Further from the water, the footprints can remain longer but later in the day, they will be but a memory as the tide comes in. The days of our lives are like footprints in the sand. They last for a moment but soon, they will be just memories.

And just like footprints in the sand, we have days that last in the crevices of the soul but there are also days that disappear as soon as they come. There are days that are filled with sunshine and abounding with love and joy. But there are also days when the sky is dark, the rain falls hard, and the blinding sand is kicked up by swirling winds. There are days that heaven seems to graze earth and there are days that the wounds run deep like those from the cuts of a thousand broken seashells. All and all, they make up the days of our lives. They're all worth it if we're in the company of the people we love.

I remember a dream I once had of walking on a beach alone. It was a beautiful day and the water was calm. I came to the edge of the waves and looked across the ocean. At the distance, I could make out a sandbar. It looked peaceful and serene. The water looked shallow and I wondered if I could wade through it to get to the sandbar. I wondered how it really was like once I got there. I also wondered how the beach would look from the vantage point of the sandbar. Then I woke up. I never knew how difficult it would be to cross the water.

My father was just diagnosed with terminal cancer. I'm making plans to fly up north to see him soon. I'm witnessing a friend facing stage 4 cancer that she named "beast." I had the end-of-life discussions with several of my patients this week. One of them asked me to say a prayer and it took all I had to mutter a few coherent words because I was overcome by his and his wife's acts of courage and grace. I put myself in their footsteps and wondered how I would feel if my footprints in the sand would soon end because I came close to the water edge and my destiny directed me to wade through the shallow water to the sandbar and never come back. I really don't know how my dad, my friend, and my patients are feeling but I think I fear dying more than I fear death. I fear for the pain that my family and friends may have because of my absence, and I fear that my wife and children won't have anyone to care for them like I can. I realize that I don't fear death. I just fear "not living."

We all can imagine what we'll see when we leave our footprints behind and arrive at the sandbar. My imagination is that it's not a sandbar after all. It's the most beautiful beach where no eye has seen, no ear has heard of, and no mind has imagined and it stretches from and to eternity. On this beach stand the loved ones who have gone before us as they are waiting for us and they look angelic beyond description. Among them also are the people whom we may have impacted in our life journeys. And walking up to us from the crowd is a radiant figure that emanates grace and love. From His lips come, "Welcome home, Son (Daughter)! We have been waiting for you. Thank you for trusting me in good times and bad ones. Thank you for not denying me but standing up for me and sharing my Word. Thank you also for doubting me or shouting anger at me at times because it showed that at those times, you still had feelings for me. At all time, I was walking with you in spirit. But now, you can walk with me in person. I have and do and will always love you. Come join your family in heaven but before you do so, look back across the water for a moment. See the loved ones you left behind on earth? Don't worry, I have been walking with them as well. They are in the palms of my hands as you were. They're mine just as you are. They will be fine. They will join the rest of us some day. Now come and rest in my Heavenly realm. I'm sorry for the struggle and suffering that you endured as you waded through the water to get here. It is at those times that it's not your footprints but your heart prints that were seen. Well done on your temporary earthly journey; now let's start the eternal one with me."

God's words will not be exactly like those because no human imagination can do justice for His holy words, but I believe their essence will be something like that.

Tomorrow will be another day. I will be leaving footprints in the sand as my life journey continues. But I will worry less on how the footprints will look and more on how the heart prints will be on the people I come across because it's not my footprints but it's those people whom I may again see in eternity. I will rejoice in the company of the ones I love and be comforted by the spirit of the One who loves me. Footprints are meant to be temporary. But heart prints are everlasting.

April, 2018

"When you saw only one set of footprints,
It was then that I carried you."

— From "Footprints in the Sand" poem

A BLADE OF GRASS

Be a free thinker and avoid following trends. Trends are just what they are: here today, gone tomorrow. A blade of grass is better than a field of weeds.

Be a listener in every conflict. Because when we listen, we already prove to the other side that we are thoughtful and reasonable.

Be a doer if we want to change the world. Everyone has an opinion, but only doers make them count.

Be a warrior on our knees before we rise to face our enemy on our feet. Because we'll find God's strength on our knees and won't just rely on our own on our feet.

Be a soft voice when everyone else screams and yells. A gentle wind of truth is more powerful than a storm of lies.

Be a giver in a world full of takers. Giving brings us joy while taking will ultimately bring grief if what we take is not ours.

Be a lover in a world that makes it easier to hate. Loving brings us closer to God while hating separates us from Him.

Appreciate what we have and not envy for what we don't. We all are given just enough to make our marks in this world. Having more than we need may just weigh us down and slow us up on where God wants us to go.

A blade of grass can someday become a pasture where streams run through and dreams are fulfilled if we stay true to ourselves and true to the Word.

"Be who you are and say what you feel, because those who mind don't matter, and those who matter don't mind."

– Bernard M. Baruch

A Good Bottle of Wine
and a Table for Four

A common phrase you may hear in the wine country of Northern California such as Sonoma or Napa valley is "Happiness is a bottle of good wine and a table for four." At first, you may think these Californians take their wines way too seriously and life seems revolve around the best blend of wine for the particular mood or food of the moment. But though taking their wines seriously since wine making is their passion and their way of life, there seems to be something more intangible but more beautiful than that. Ask anyone working in a vine-yard about their brand of wine and, for a moment, you become their best friend. They will stop momentarily and talk about the uniqueness of their wines but sooner or later, they will talk about the uniqueness of their families and friends and fellow wine makers and the love and the pride they have for each other. It's about relationship! Yes, a good bottle of wine is the means but the reason for a table for four is the desire to share, to love and laugh together with a group of friends or family or even strangers. Life seems to slow down a bit there and you won't see many people looking at their phone messages or taking "selfies" at every turn. If not working, they seem to prefer looking across the table and engage in hearty conversations and share whatever there is on the table including that bottle of wine. It is all about relationship even though it may look like a bottle of good wine and a table for four, or six or more.

Our relationship with God is a little bit like that. He longs for us to slow down a bit in our hectic life to sit across a table from Him. He loves for us to engage with Him our heart desires, our fears and joy and yes, even our anger towards Him. And the wine He brought to share is the best because it's the blood of His own Son, the One we called Jesus. His desire is for us to have a happy and abundant life even though it doesn't always seem to be so.

Happiness is a good bottle of wine and a table for four or even for two if the one sitting across the table is the one we love. It's all about relationship and the Californians in the wine country seem to know and to live it well.

Image by Christine Ponchia from Pixabay

"And wine to gladden the heart of man, oil to make his face shine and bread to strengthen man's heart."

– PSALM 104:15, ESV

THE COMPLEXITIES OF GRAPES

The Napa Valley in Northern California has some of the best vineyards and therefore produces some of the best wines in the world, rivaling those from southern France or from Tuscany, Italy. The soil condition, caused by a mixture of volcanic ash from the eruption of Mount Helena millions of years ago and a perfect combination of iron, clay, sand, and other minerals combined with the cool breeze from the Pacific ocean and ample sunshine makes this area ideal for vineyards.

But do you know the weather there is not always perfect for the grape vines to produce bountiful harvest of grapes every year? Just like farmers, vineyard owners are at the mercy of Mother Nature to determine their livelihood. However, unlike a farm crop, grapevines have a unique ability to "weather" adverse conditions. If the weather is harsh, these vines will PERSEVERE and survive and produce about half the amount of grapes as they normally would in perfect weather condition. The beautiful fact is though the amount of grapes is less, the quality of these grapes is superior to those produced in more ideal weather. In the vernacular of the winemakers, these grapes have more "complexities" or in other words, more CHARACTER and therefore will be made into more quality wines. I was told that this is nature's way of preserving the vines, as better grapes, though less abundant in amount, will attract more birds to consume them and thus scatter the seeds and HOPE to enhance their chance for preservation in tough times and to produce more grapes later.

I think humans are very much the same. In difficult times, the human spirit can rise above adversity and help us PERSEVERE and some of our best works often are born out of difficult trials. In tough times, we are more focused, more determined, less complacent, and much more appreciative of the little things that we have. In other words, adverse conditions can produce in us more CHARACTER. This is when we learn that the quality of anything in life is better than its quantity and it is with the building of CHARACTER that we HOPE that we're ready to move on to the next level in life that God intends for us to be.

So trials in life, though difficult, can be exactly what we need so we can grow more abundantly. Someone has said that we shouldn't ask God to deliver us from difficult times but to help us get through them. This fact about the grapevine helps me understand Romans 5:3-4 better.

Image by Jill Wellington from Pixabay

"Because we know that suffering produces PERSEVERANCE; PERSEVERANCE, CHARACTER; and CHARACTER, HOPE."

– ROMANS 5:3–4, NIV

Love, Time, and Dimension

I love science fiction! I watched a science fiction movie *"Interstellar"* while working out a few years ago. I was so spellbound by the movie that I found myself watching it more than working out. It is a story about planet Earth that is dying and a group of scientists have to travel to the far reaches of space to look for an alternative planet. The problem is that due to the vast dimension of space and due to the law of relativity, an hour in space is like years on earth, so even if their mission is successful, they might not get back to earth on time to save their loved ones. Faced with insurmountable odds and having to choose their options with the limited data they have, Brand, a mission specialist (played by Anne Hathaway) and Cooper, the pilot (Matthew McConnaughey), argued over the choices. At one point, Brand uttered the most unscientific statement, "Love is the only thing that transcends time and dimension. Maybe we should follow it, though we don't understand it." That is also the most profound statement in the whole movie. I won't tell you the rest of the story, except that in the end, it is love that saves humanity.

A couple of thousand years ago, the apostle Paul wrote the same thing in Romans 8:38 regarding God's love that saved humanity, "For I am convinced that neither death nor life, neither angels nor demons, neither the present nor the future, nor any powers, neither height nor depth, nor anything else in all creations, will be able to separate us from the love of God that is in Christ Jesus our Lord." I truly believe that our love for each other can and God's love for us does transcend time and dimension.

Image by Lumina Obscura from Pixabay

"For I am convinced that neither death nor life … nor anything else in all creations, will be able to separate us from the love of god that is in Christ Jesus our Lord."
– ROMANS 8:38, NIV

Good and Evil

Evil kills, steals, and destroys. God saves, provides, and restores. Evil resorts to hatred, division, chaos, and destruction. God exalts love, unity, peace, and edification.

Evil uses race, sex, income inequality or whatever he can to divide and conquer. God sees through our differences and looks at the only things that matter: our hearts toward Him and each other.

But there is one thing evil and God has in common. God sees no color. Neither does evil. We all are equal opportunity victims of evil no matter what our race is and he diligently seeks us. We also share the same equality when it comes to God's love and He desperately pursues us.

The human heart is not an empty vessel. It is at any one time or another, either filled with the spirit of God or with the essence evil. It is up to us to choose. The struggles in our world often start with the battle in our hearts.

The good news is in the next world, good will have already triumphed over evil. In the meantime, in our current world that seems to spiral out of control, we have to kneel and ask God daily for guidance then stand up and do what is good.

"The thief comes only to steal and kill and destroy; I have come that they may have life, and have it to the full."

– JOHN 10:10, NIV

THIS OLD BARN

There is this old barn right off Al 65 in Hollytree, between Paint Rock and Skyline, Alabama. I passed it many times driving from Hampton Cove to Skyline. The barn is very run-down. On the best day, it looks like a heap of ruins. The wooden walls are rotted and are falling apart at places. The tin roof is rusted and threatening to cave in. I often wondered why it hadn't been torn down and rebuilt. This morning, however, it caught my attention and the view was so stunning that I stopped my car and took a good look and a picture of it.

The barn stood out against the backdrop of the Alabama blue sky in spring time. White clouds were outlined by radiant sun rays streaming down from heaven. Green grass, fueled by the rainstorm from a couple of nights ago, grew tall and gently swayed by the cool breeze. Wild yellow blooms canvassed large swaths of the landscape. At a distance, cows were seen lazily basking in the pasture. Little birds were frolicking in the puddle of water close to the barn and the sweet smell of damp earth filled the air. What a beautiful sight it was. This was rural Alabama. It was a piece of Americana and in my humble opinion, it was one of God's most beautiful creations. And the old barn? Without it, I don't believe the landscape would have been as magnificent. It added the rustic beauty that only an old, run-down barn could.

Claude Monet, the French impressionist, would have loved this barn. Living in Giverny, a little town in the countryside near Paris in the late 1800s to early 1900s, Monet converted his barn to an art studio. There, he painted such masterpieces as the *Water Lilies and Japanese Bridge*, the subjects of which were—and still are—on his property. He called Giverny "a little piece of heaven." The barn and the Alabama countryside I saw this morning must be someone's little piece of heaven. It certainly had a certain endearing beauty.

As I drove off, I hoped the owner of the barn would never tear it down. Sometimes, it's the imperfections that make things perfect!

I also reflected on our human experience as I left the place. Just like this old barn, we are all flawed and there are parts of us that are best not seen or in need of renovation. Some of us suffer even more brokenness than others. Some are divorced, facing depression, loneliness, addiction or fighting chronic and even terminal illnesses. Some are grieving from the recent or not so recent losses of loved ones. We don't know why bad things happen to good people other than we're living in a fallen world and these things happen. But we find comfort in the belief our Creator will right all wrongs in the afterlife and what are lost will be repaid. "In the meantime, we need to be reassured that, of all God's creations, we are His most treasured! Broken or not, we are His "masterpiece." Just like the old barn I marveled at this morning, our imperfections are what make us "perfect" in His love

April 2016

"Through the ample open door of the peaceful country barn, a sun-lit pasture field, with cattle and horses feeding; And haze, and vista, and the far horizon, fading away."

– Walt Whitman

LANDSCAPE PHOTOGRAPHY

I recently picked up landscape photography as a hobby. Just a few months ago, terminology such as aperture, shutter speed, and ISO were all foreign to me. Now, I understand they are camera settings that either allow how much light to enter through the camera lens or how sensitive the camera sensor is set to receive it. A good photographer would judge what the appropriate settings should be under each lighting condition to produce an image with the best color display and resolution. With the right composition and theme, the images produced can indeed be works of art. So whenever I can, I find myself in the middle of nature dialing in the camera settings, pointing the camera at a landscape in front of me, holding my breath, pressing the shutter button and voila, what comes back on the image display is ... well, not exactly a work of art. Let's just say I often delete most of the pictures I take and photoshop the heck out of the rest to make them halfway presentable. I have much to learn.

But landscape photography reminds me how magnificent an artist and how real God is. Sunrises and sunsets remind me that our God is a God of rhythm and faithfulness. He is mystical like the morning mist emerging from the surface of still water. He is gentle like the wind that scatters the white floaties from a dandelion in the fields. Overarching trees and billowing clouds that cast their reflections on the golden pond below is a display or his artistry. Butterflies and bumblebees flirting with the young flowers that blush in the colors of spring is an example of his passion. His love for relationship is seen in a pair of ducks frolicking next to a wooden bridge and sharing the glistening pond with the busy coy fish below. His randomness is obvious in a leaf floating atop a stream of playful currents of a creek in the woods. But his desire for boundaries is also evident in the fences bordering green pastures where cattle graze under the blue sky of early spring and a looming mountain range at the distance that brackets the lush landscape of the countryside. He is a God of grandeur whenever the stars of heaven captivate one's heart or the great canyons that amaze one's eyes. But he is a God of details whenever tiny flowers are seen amongst the young blades of grass that are still dressed in the droplets of the morning due.

And the most amazing reminder of landscape photography to me is that despite the beauty and majesty of His creations in front of my camera lens, the one He values most is the person behind it. Among His vast works of art, we are His most cherished. What's even more astounding is on a good day, in many ways I am, and I suspect you are, so imperfect but He still cares. Physically and spiritually I am flawed, grainy, underexposed, and poorly composed. It would take a heck of photoshopping of Godly proportion to make me halfway presentable and yet He cares. He loves and cares for you and I just the way we are, warts and all, and sins and all. The aperture of His heart is big enough to forgive. The shutter speed of His love is fast enough to forget. And the ISO of His sensor is exquisite enough to hear our prayers. And that ... makes God both the best camera and the best photographer of all.

"Photography is a way of feeling, of touching, of loving. What you have caught on film is captured forever....It remembers little things, long after you have forgotten everything."

– Aaron Siskind

CHAPTER 7

VALLEYS AMONG THE FIELDS

AMAZING GRACE

It has been a few years since my friend went home with the Lord. I was consulted to see him about five years ago at a hospital where I worked when he was admitted for hemolytic anemia, a complication of lupus. Weakened and pale, he gave me an account of his past history and the symptoms that led to this hospital admission. Then with a brilliant smile, he thanked me for seeing him and he thanked God for being in the hospital! As I walked away, I was perplexed by his praise of God's "favor," in the depth of his illness and during one of the worst times of his life. Little did I know as I left that hospital room that Kris would become one of my best friends, my mentor, and my Christian hero.

Moving to Huntsville, Alabama, from Detroit to take care of his mother, Kris developed kidney failure from lupus and became disabled. After a period of kidney dialysis, he received a renal transplant which he was always grateful for and considered it God's "favor." But after a period of calm weather, the storm came in the form of hemolytic anemia, the final complication that ultimately took his life.

I once asked Kris why he praised God for His "favor" every time he was hospitalized. His response was because it gave him the opportunity to minister to the doctors, nurses, and ancillary staff that took care of him.

In our clinic, Kris would come early to his appointments so he could spend time to "fellowship" with everyone he ran into and talked about God's grace in his life. He held a devotional study and formed a prayer circle at an outpatient center every time he went there for blood transfusion and talked about God's grace. Though disabled from his illness, Kris volunteered to cook for the Soup Kitchen, a ministry that feeds the homeless. He saw it as a privilege to help care for those who were less fortunate than he was. I had the pleasure of accompanying Kris on a couple of his grocery shopping trips for the Soup Kitchen. Barely able to walk, but somewhere between canned foods and eggs, he would talk about God's grace. Kris loved food! He invited me to Ryan's restaurant for lunch prior to one of these grocery shopping outings, and between the fried chicken and collard greens, he paused and talked about God's grace. A month before his death, I invited Kris to a Vietnamese restaurant. I introduced him to "bun thit nuong," one of my favorites. It was Vermicelli noodle that's underlined by a layer of shredded cucumber and carrots, topped with grilled pork, sprinkled with grounded and roasted peanuts, and adorned by a pinch of mint then bathed with a generous portion of sweetened fish sauce. It was an instant hit to Kris! He partook the dish with passion then between the noodle and the grilled meats he ... you guessed it, talked about God's grace.

He loved his family. He cared for his elderly mother and talked about his daughter frequently. He was also reunited with the love of his life about one year before his death. They were to marry and I was to be one of his groomsmen. Of course, this marriage was to be a huge "favor" from God and he was in cloud nine preparing for it. But as fate would have it, Kris died two weeks before the wedding date.

One day before his death, in a hospital ICU, I told Kris it's all right to go home to his Heavenly Father. I told him he didn't have to struggle anymore and I would no longer try to hold him back. Though still in pain, he responded with a brilliant smile, the same smile I saw the first time I met him three years prior and the same smile that was his trademark to those who knew him.

His Christian life is the one I try to emulate because there was no debate on any Christian theology. There was no discussion on where and when to go to church or which denomination was most sensible. It modeled most closely to the Jesus' teachings that I know: love your God and love your neighbors. It was that simple. There was no pretense and no condition. It's about praising God in all circumstances and being of service to others, especially the ones less fortunate than we are. In Kris' case, his life was often about others' wellbeing more than his own, and he never tried to draw attention to his illness.

I missed you, my brother! The next time I see you again, somewhere in heaven, let's find a Vietnamese restaurant. I'll ask for a table and let's order "bun thit nuong". You won't need to talk about God's grace this time. We'll pull up another chair and invite Jesus to join us. This time, I will thank Jesus myself of the amazing grace he had on my life, one of which was to know you! Rest in peace, my friend!

"My grace is sufficient for you, for my power is made perfect in weakness."

– 2 CORINTHIANS 12:9, NIV

Under Your Wings

S he spends most of her day foraging for insects and worms to feed her chicks. Not long ago, the hatchlings broke through the shells and started crying for food. Now a little older and bigger but still blind and featherless, the baby chicks demand even more nutrients to grow. High on a canopy of the forest is home, a nest she had labored to build, which now houses the most important things in her life: the baby chicks. Under her wings, they find safety and from her beak is the sustenance that quenches their hunger. She will protect them with her life and until they are old enough to fly away, and her whole existence now is devoted to their wellbeing.

She will take flight as the day dawns to hunt for food and returns with each catch to feed the hungry mouths and will tirelessly do so until sunset. She braves the elements and eludes larger predatory birds daily with one singular purpose in mind and that is to ensure the survival of her youngs. When the night comes, she will rest next to them and under her wings they fall asleep. She will glance at the stars and soon her eyes close momentarily until the dawning of the next day. At sunrise, she will again take flight and the endless cycle of hunting and feeding continues. Not all days are calm and peaceful. The storms can rage and forest fires may loom too close. In those moments, under her wings is where the young chicks will find refuge.

God's love for His children is like that of the mother bird. His love is also like that of a single parent raising his or her children. It is unconditional and tireless. There are few things in life more difficult and yet more admirable than raising one's children as a single parent. God means for each of us to travel in our journeys as a team. But once a family is broken and one parent is missing, the journey is even more arduous and the full load of parenting can fall on the shoulders of the other one. To all the single parents out there, please continue your journeys with your heads held high and hearts filled with the love of your youngs and spirits lifted with the love of God and also with our admiration. When the night comes and when your children are asleep and the enemy attacks you with doubt and loneliness, just remember that "the One in you is greater than the one in the world" and "weeping may endure for a night but joy comes in the morning." Those words may sound like clichés but they are actually God's truth. Just like your children finding refuge under your wings, find refuge under His. There will come a day that your personal life will be fully restored and your sacrifice will be fully repaid. In the meantime, find peace in the knowledge that because of you, your children (or perhaps grandchildren) can grow up to be what God destined them to be and because of you, though the storms and fires in their lives may come, they will feel safe and protected.

When your own trials come or when you feel the burden is too much to bear, lean on Jesus and He will give you rest. He promises that His yoke is easy and His burden is light. When your hardship comes, soar as high as your wingspan can take you and show others that you are a child of God with all of His strength, courage, and determination. Under your wings is the promise of a new generation and the promise of a better tomorrow. Under your wings is where God places His trust.

Image by Gerhard Gellinger from3 Pixabay

"He will cover you with his feathers. He will shelter you with his wings. His faithful promise are your armor and protection."

– Psalm 91:4, NIV

MODERN-DAY SLAVERY

She is underage but in her world, age loses its innocence early.
She has a unique face, but she might as well be faceless.
She was born with an identity, but in her line of "work," she
is called by many names.
She has a family but they have not seen her for so long and
they wonder if she still exists.
She has a callused heart because it has been shattered too
many times.
She is a timid soul because her spirit is being held captive.
She feels unloved in the arms of lovers that bought her
for a night or two.
She has no other choice because predators know how to
siphon off her resistance.
She is a commodity, existing solely for the purpose of short
term trading in the meat market.
She is just a shell of her former self, a mannequin that hides
what is truly hers.
She used to be her own, but she now is a slave in a world that
doesn't know slavery still exists.

She lives in a shadow that awaits a light to outshine darkness
and goodness that can overcome evil.
She is a flower that withers but you can bring sunshine and
restore her essence.

She is just one example of many female and male victims of human trafficking, the modern-day slavery that is an extraordinarily profitable industry around the world. Yes, it is also profitable in our country as well and in my home state Alabama, I-20 is known as the superhighway of sex trafficking in the USA. Text the National Human Trafficking Hotline at 233733 or call the toll-free hotline at 1-888-373-7888 to report potential human trafficking.

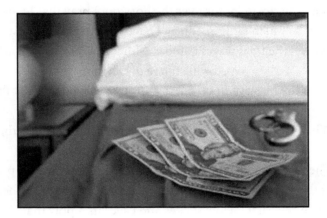

"People were created to be loved. Things were created to be used. The reason why the world is in chaos is because things are being loved and people are being used."

– Author unknown

WHEN DARKNESS DESCENDS

When darkness descends, I pray that Your light will shine on
my path.
When the storm looms over the horizon, I pray that I have at
least as much faith in You as I have fear for the unknown.
When the tidal waves come crashing in, I pray that Your
Word will still be my anchor.
When the massive flood breaks through the dam, I pray that
Your saving grace will keep me afloat.
When the heat of the scorching fire consumes my breath, I
pray that Your water will quench my thirst.
When I'm stranded by the worst blizzard of the winter, I pray
that the promise of Your salvation is enough to warm my heart.
When the earth below shakes and caves in, I pray that Your
loving hand will hold on to mine.
When the mountain above rumbles and crumbles, I pray that
in Your mercy I will find my refuge.
When I'm thrown into the cold and unforgiving wilderness, I
pray that Your spirit will whisper to me the right way home.
When the enemy comes charging forth, I pray that You will
give me the courage to face it head on.

When I am in the valley of shadow of death, I pray that You
will walk by my side and I will fear no evil.
When I am in the depth of despair, I pray that You will hear
my voice, even if I can't hear Yours.
When the angel of death returns, I will proclaim my victory
in You. Because in You, no matter what happens here on
earth, I have already won the battle against my foe.

Let's pray with and for all the patients who are facing recurrent cancers and for those who are suffering from great losses recently. Let
them know that they are not fighting their battles alone. We'll stay with
them when their darkness descends and help them we will until their
morning comes.

"From the ends of the earth I call to you, I call as my heart
grows faint; lead me to the rock that is higher than I."
– PSALM 61:2, NIV

WHEN THE TWILIGHT DIMS

Imagine living on a desolate island where the sun never rises. The sky is starless and the only light in the horizon is the twilight of the day that never comes. The only sound comes from the howling of the wind atop the dunes and the monotonous crashing of the waves as they come ashore. There are no living creatures around and every day is like the last. The water is cold and the sand is wet. Imagine being condemned to the place where there is no hope for rescue and there is no joy in the lifeless existence. Then one day, even the twilight dims.

Imagine sitting in a crowded room that's filled with noisy conversations but no one can hear you or crossing a busy street but no one knows you're there as you are all but invisible. Then one day, even the room is empty and the street is deserted.

Imagine the only relationship you have is an abused one. With it, your self-worth is nominal and without it, your identity is nonexistent. Then one day your cry is silenced.

Imagine the weight of the world is upon you and with every step it seems heavier. Imagine your dream is dashed, your fortune's collapsed, and your name is smeared from here to eternity. Your friends have abandoned you, your enemies are out for blood, and your family has turned its back. Then one day, fleeing from it all seems like a logical escape.

Imagine having a pain that's relentless and every waking moment is a struggle to survive and no matter how hard you try otherwise, the only way you know to end this pain is by ending life itself.

Though death is not the desired destination, living in pain or loneliness or rejection or in shame is no longer the desired journey. Feeling like a burden to loved ones is no longer an acceptable option. Ending life becomes an alluring escape.

Depression and the sense of hopelessness know no mercy and spare no segment of society. They are as pervasive as they are insidious. No fame nor fortune nor nobility of birth would be enough to escape their grasp. They are the cancers of the soul. They can be treated and mitigated, but they're not always easy to cure. Like victims of cancers who can succumb to the illness from within their bodies, victims from suicide are not to be blamed for succumbing also to the illness or desperation from within their souls.

Having lost a brother who chose to end his life rather than living a "meaningless existence" as he called it, I know how devastating the aftermath can be for those he left behind. For some time, life lost a little luster when he's gone, but life did go on for our family. There were of course the regrets that we didn't recognize any warning signs earlier. But for the rest of us, we just learned to love each other more and try to see each other regularly, at least once a year at our family reunion. That's how we cope with his loss.

In a society that's increasingly more engrossed in social media than personal interaction, we are losing the true human connection. In a political climate that encourages bashing each other for having a different viewpoint, where the mainstream media is hopelessly biased and political parties are more concerned about consolidating their bases than working together for the good of all, we are losing our identity as one nation under God. In a country where death from suicide exceeds 40,000 a year, there is an inherent problem that needs not be ignored.

The solution to a complexed and multifaceted problem like suicide is not a simple one and certainly there is not a one-size-fits-all remedy. But perhaps, it can start within our hearts and souls. It can start by recognizing each other as being uniquely made by our Creator in His image and part of our responsibilities is to lift each other up in times of need. It starts by our willingness to step into someone's life and help get them the proper care and assistance when we recognize that their world is caving in. It starts by listening without judging. And it continues by having an honest dialogue when conflict arises and trying to solve it in a way that no one gets hurt. It starts from families that pray together and play together. It continues when civility is brought back to the public forum. It starts when prayers of all faiths are allowed back in school and saying the Pledge of Allegiance is not forbidden. It continues by putting God back in government as this nation was founded under His precepts and it continues when worshiping God and saluting the American flag are not seen as gestures of exclusivity but of both unity and freedom. It starts by enforcing the policy of zero tolerance when it comes to bullying or abuse and continues with God's greatest commandment, "Love thy neighbors," in and out of our workplaces. It starts by doing life together and continues by serving or helping those less fortunate than we are. It starts by teaching our children what's right and wrong and continues by respecting law and order. It starts by asking for help when we're in trouble and continues by offering help to those who are in trouble. It starts by recognizing that life is a gift and it continues by realizing that there is a purpose for every life. Maybe, just maybe when civility and morality and compassion and awareness of each other's plights are brought back to our society, depression and suicide rate may decline or at least become more manageable. In the end, God's light can cast out all darkness if we're willing to let it enter our hearts and souls and to be His lighthouses. Let's strive to live not just in our own world but be the source of light that guides those who live in darkness to see their ways out. When the twilight from the horizon dims, darkness can be broken by that which emerges from a lighthouse.

If you are or if you know someone in crisis: call the toll-free National Suicide Prevention Lifeline (NSPL) at 1–800–273–TALK (8255), 24 hours a day, 7 days a week. The service is available to everyone.

"What the caterpillar calls the end of the world, the master calls a butterfly."

– Author unknown

OVER THE WAVES

A female seagull is awakened by the sound of the waves and her feathers are gently ruffled by the morning breeze as she emerges from the dunes. A flock of pelicans are already in formation in search for small fishes as they skim over the water. Sand crabs scurry around as the sun declares a new day over the horizon. The tide has retreated, revealing on the sand nearby a fresh carpet of various seashells in their morning glory. But the sky is overcast today and the chill from the previous night is still lingering. She slowly walks to edge of the water then longingly looks over the waves as if her mate, at any moment now, will appear from the distance to meet her on the beach. She has seen him in her dream. But like the previous mornings, it was just a dream as he has been gone awhile. Sometimes she thought she heard his call, but it was from another. Sometimes she thought she saw his shadow on the sand, but as she turned her head, it was just a stranger passing by.

As a couple, they had weathered many storms together. They also shared life's most precious moments from sunrises to sunsets until one day, as fate would have it, her life companion fell from grace and succumbed to a devastating illness.

Her sorrow has been as deep as an endless hollow and as vast as the greatest of oceans. But it's during the night when the sea is quiet and the moon hides behind the clouds that loneliness becomes her most formidable enemy. It is then that life is teetering at the edge of hopelessness and joy is as elusive as the reflection of light on the water's surface during a moonless night.

Today, like any other day, she will have to summon enough will to fly over the waves in search of sustenance. There is less zeal in her to take flight today, but take flight alone she must, because there are others who still need her here. As she soars over the waves, resting below and hidden amongst the tall grass of the dunes is a nest that houses three little hungry mouths that await her return.

Like this sea bird, some of us are still grieving the loss of loved ones today. May we remind each other that losses are only temporary, and over the waves and beyond the horizon is a world of eternal life and eventual reunion. Until such time, let's find joy in serving and in being each other's company. Over the waves of sorrow, we'll keep soaring.

"And the God of all grace, who called you to His eternal glory in Christ, after you have suffered a little while, will himself restore you and make you strong, firm and steadfast."

– 1 PETER 5:10, NIV

YOUR WILL

When the sky turns dark, I praise You anyway for remaining the Light within me. When the current is strong, I praise You anyway for giving me the strength not to go under. When the rain falls hard, I praise You anyway for sheltering me from the flood. When the waves are unforgiving, I praise You anyway for teaching me to trust You to calm the storm.

When my cup is not full, I praise You anyway for blessing me with a cup. When my heart is broken, I praise You anyway for blessing me with a heart to love. When my soul feels burdened, I praise You anyway for without You, I'm soulless. When my plan does not work out, I praise You anyway because I know You have a better plan for us. When my will is not Yours, I praise You anyway because in the eternal scheme of things, Your will is what matters.

Your will matters not just because You are God, but because the basis of Your will is ... love.

June 2018

Image from Abel Escobar from Pixabay

"Here's what I'm learning about God: God is more intent on perfecting us through trouble than protecting us from trouble."

– Bruce W. Martin, author, speaker, teacher

OUR VOTES

She is a middle-aged mother of three. The furrows on her forehead, the calluses on her hands, and her less-than-perfect posture are telltales of a hard life. Her husband has been incarcerated for drug trafficking and petty crimes to fund his own habits for a number of years and has not contributed to their livelihood. Living in a small town in Alabama, she manages to raise her children by working at a local gas station at night and cleaning houses during the day. Their home is a broken-down trailer on the outskirt of town. Their meals are what she can afford with a meager income, often supplemented with what she can get from the food pantry of the nearby Care Center. Every Christmas, her oldest daughter would unfold the tiny Christmas tree from the storage closet and decorated it with whatever string lights that still worked and a few mismatched ornaments. And the presents under the Christmas trees, at least the good ones, would come from the benevolence of a church from an adjacent and more affluent town. She goes to work in a clunker that spews more black smoke than a paper mill chimney can. Most of her and her children's clothes come from a thrift store down the road from the gas station.

Her oldest daughter will graduate from high school in a few months and plans to attend a community college across the Tennessee

River some 40 miles away. This daughter will have to work her way through college but she will be the first from both sides of the family to seek higher education.

Immensely proud of the daughter's goal to break the cycle of poverty and make a life for herself, this mother has been saving a small sum of money over the last year-and-a-half. She wants to buy her daughter a car as a graduation gift and as a means for her to go to college.

So on this Saturday morning, she drove to a used car lot the next town over. Pretty much all the vehicles she looked at were over her budget. Feeling discouraged, she began to walk back to her own clunker when she spotted a couple of cars away from the others with the prices written on their windshields that were just a little above what she could afford. Her heart was filled with joy and hope. Perhaps she could barter with the dealership. One was a rusted old Chevy with the Dixie flag painted on the roof and the silhouette of a naked female figure etched on the rear window. Its appearance would likely offend somebody. She later learned from the car salesman that the owner was an amateur mechanic and had rebuilt the engine, so the car would run fine. The other choice was an old Ford sedan with a fresh coat of paint. It was definitely more aesthetically appealing but the asking price was low for a reason. It was involved in a multi-car pileup and it too had been rebuilt. The electrical system was short-circuited and had to be rewired, and the nice appearance belies an unreliable engine. She had returned to this dealership several times since the first encounter, every Saturday morning that she's off from work, to consider the options and negotiate for the buy. On the last day, with all the cash she has in her purse, she stands in front of the cars one more time to make the final selection, when a couple of salesmen walk by on the way to their office. Though unintended, she can overhear one of them say, "I can't believe the redneck's vehicle is still here. Which lowlife would even look at it? It's time to sell it for scrap." The other salesman replies, "Yeah, but at least it runs. The other piece of junk looks good but is untrustworthy. Which fool would want to buy it"?" Her heart momentarily sinks. She's the lowlife fool who for weeks has thought long and hard to make a choice on a gift that she works so hard for, to give to a daughter that she loves and is so proud of. Holding back her tears, she holds her head high and with purse in tow, she walks to the dealership sales office to make an offer.

Our nation is a little like this loving mother. We are weaker and poorer with a stagnant economy. Unemployment rate is high and those who are fortunate enough to work find ourselves with lower median income and soaring insurance premiums. We're more divided politically, racially, and religiously. More youths are seen stepping on our flag and some athletes gain notoriety for disrespecting our national anthem. Inner city shooting deaths are climbing while politicians argue where to put the blame. Sanctuary cities hide illegal alien criminals while our veterans die waiting for medical care or live on the streets. Cops are targeted for murder while trying to protect the people who demonstrate against them. The threat of terrorism is increasingly looming within and without our porous border.

Religious liberty is increasingly threatened as political correctness permeates and overshadows our society. We're leaving our children with a crushing interest from a huge national debt as we continue to borrow from foreign countries with questionable human right records thanks to the ineptitude of our government.

But this November, we will have the opportunity to vote. The choice we make is a gift we'll leave for our children. Our presidential candidates' visions for America are vastly different and their policies will lead this nation to a divergent course, depending who we vote into office. We have two very flawed candidates when it comes to personality traits. But like the poor mother, we have no other choices. The biased media and political pundits and the social elites and celebrities have been telling us who to vote for and demonize the other all day long. The differences in the candidates' policies are often buried under the personal garbage dug up by the surrogates of each side.

We will hold our heads high and hold back our tears if we have to when we go to vote this November. Voting is a privilege that many generations of men and women have died to gift to us and it will be a gift we leave for the next generation. We pray that God will continue to bless this great nation no matter who we vote into office as He has since its inception. When America is strong and prosperous, the whole world benefits. When it falters, so does the rest of the free world. God bless America! God bless our world!

October 2016

"If my people, who are called by my name, will humble themselves and pray and seek my face and turn from their wicked ways, then I will hear from heaven, and forgive their sin and will heal their land."

– 2 CHRONICLES 7:14, NIV

A Bridge to the Other Side

Tonight, I called and conveyed my condolence to a grieving mother who, earlier this morning, lost her son to a terminal illness. It was a task that I had done many times but never got good at, and the task never got any easier no matter how long I have been doing it. In my opinion, there is no greater love on earth than that of a mother to her child and consequently, there is no greater pain when the child is forever lost. Through her tears and with her voice trembling in sadness and exhaustion, she thanked us for our service. As I tried to comfort her, it is her words that comforted me. "I am blessed to have him for twenty-two years" and "He was such a sweet son" but "he is home with Jesus now," and "I believe I will see him again someday" were what she expressed. There is so much dignity in that and there was so much love and devotion that this mother gave her son in his six months' battle with terminal cancer. But I also saw or heard of the love, devotion, and professionalism from the nursing and ancillary staff at our cancer center, a hospice agency, and at the local hospitals where he spent many of the last few months of his life. I observed the loving care, the comforting touch, the gentle smile these caretakers had for this young man during his darkest hours. And privately, I also observed their anguish and heartbreaks as his course continued to deteriorate despite our best efforts. As his health declined and as he was gripped with depression and wish for seclusion, one of the oncology nurses successfully pulled him out of "the pit" by convincing him to go on movie dates with her! What a beautiful act of kindness that was. She did more for him than I ever could in his struggle with cancer. Collectively, this loving mother and the nursing and ancillary staff that cared for this young man formed a bridge that allowed him to cross from this world to the other side with as much dignity and comfort as possible. This was a bridge of love, devotion, and compassion.

So this morning, as the young man completed his journey, he slipped from the loving arms of his mother and family and friends to the loving arms of God. He did so by gently walking across this bridge. He never fell helplessly to the abyss.

Hippocrates, the Greek physician, over two thousand years ago proclaimed the heart of health care vocation as "to cure a few, to treat often, to comfort always." When it comes to terminal illness, not much has changed since. We as health care providers don't get to choose who we can save. That task belongs to God. But we still get to choose to "treat often and to comfort always." We get to choose to be a part of that bridge that helps our terminal patients cross to the other side with as much comfort and dignity as possible if we can't cure them. And over the last six months, I've seen that bridge so beautifully displayed in the life and death of this young man. The good news is on the other side, his suffering will end and his tears will be wiped away.

February 2016

Image by Larisa Koshkina from Pixabay

"He will wipe every tear from their eyes. There will be no more death or mourning or crying or pain, for the old order of things has passed away."

– Revelation 21:4–6, NIV

CHAPTER 8

THE MEDICAL FIELD

House Keeping

F ew know their names. Collectively, they're often referred to as "housekeeping." These ladies and a few men can be seen pushing the carts containing a collection of brooms, mops, paper towel, rags, and a variety of cleaning agents and a water bucket or two on the hospital's hallways. Every morning, they would carefully sweep and mop around the feet of the doctors and nurses at the nurse's stations, trying not to disturb the busy professionals. They quietly remove the trash, strip the linens, and disinfect the room soon after a patient is discharged so the next one from the ER can be moved in to take up residence.

You won't likely see their names on any plaques as employees of the year. Few would stop to ask how their day is going. Patients may ask to be admitted to a particular hospital because of its proximity to their homes, because it's in their insurance networks, because of their doctors' preference, maybe the nursing care is good, rarely because of the kitchen menu, but never because of an awesome housekeeping department. Raving letters from patients often thankfully mentioned the life-saving works of doctors, compassionate care from nurses, and friendly smiles from the dietary staff, but housekeepers? If mentioned at all, housekeeping is an afterthought. More often if housekeeping is in the conversation, it is about how unclean a room is. They are at the bottom of the totem pole in the hospital corporate world.

I've often seen "housekeepers" quietly pushing their carts down hospital hallways early in the morning and at strange hours of the night. At times, they would break a polite smile but most of the times their eyes cast a distant look. Perhaps, they are used to not being greeted or acknowledged. They seem content to be invisible, or are they? When asked, their stories sound all too real: a daughter fighting cancer, or a son awaiting to be released from prison, or a grandchild they're raising because both parents are too high on drugs to be ... parents. Their worries are deep and their burdens are heavy. Their problems are all too visible and can be seen in the wrinkles of their faces.

They are at the bottom of the hospital hierarchy and yet, if there is an accidental spillage of epic proportion or a loss of bowel or bladder control in a patient room, "housekeeping" can be heard over the intercom or their pagers can be heard loudly shrieking.

I recently asked two housekeeping ladies—one working at a local hospital for more than thirty-three years and the other one about seven—what kept them there so long. Their answers were the same: "patient care." They love caring for the sick as much as any other health care professionals do, perhaps even more. They're often seen helping the nurse's aides lifting or repositioning patients in their beds or helping them getting to the bathrooms, none of which is in their job description. Who else would have the fortitude to, day in and day out, pick up the soiled bedsheets, clean up bodily fluids, or wipe off the spatter of blood wherever it lands in the aftermath of a code blue? They see the indignities of the sick and helpless and they clean them up, not because they enjoy the filth and the stench but they see it as part of their job not just to make a living but also to care for another human being in the capacity few others are willing to do. To me, their job is just as important as another "skilled" health care professional. Imagine a hospital without a housekeeping function. Without the sanitizing and sterilizing works, I'm afraid E. coli and pseudomonas will set up permanent residence and wreak havoc in patient care and MRSA can be the leading cause of death in postop patients. At the very least, who would want to be admitted to a hospital that smells like a draining abscess or a stagnant sewage?

The next time we see a housekeeping person, let's return their smile with ours. Let's ask how their day is going and thank them for their service. Let's acknowledge their indispensable part in health-care profession. Let's pray for their personal struggles and invite them to pray for ours. Just like us they may not want any accolades, but acknowledgment is always a human desire and needs to be stated.

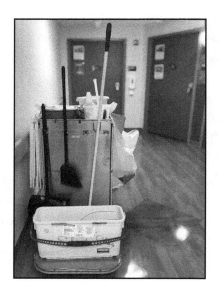

"And this mess is so big
And so deep and so tall,
We cannot pick it up.
There is no way at all!"

– Dr. Seuss, *The Cat in the Hat*

Beauty from Within

D iamond is the gem of all gemstones. Derived from the ancient Greek word "adamas" which means unbreakable, diamond is known for its superlative strength. It also epitomizes beauty, clarity, and purity. It is the jewelry that symbolizes love, commitment, social status, and wealth. But what's more impressive is how diamond is created. Just like coals, the carbon atoms that form uncut diamonds come from organic plant life or carbon-containing minerals that are buried underground and under pressure and heat for an extended period of time. But unlike coals, the depth, pressure, heat, and duration required for these carbon atoms to form strong covalent bond and arrange themselves in a perfect lattice is staggering. Most natural diamonds were formed about 100 miles below the earth's surface, in the lithospheric mantle for 1 to 3 billion years, where the carbon atoms sustained a tremendous amount of pressure and heat (2,750 degrees F) and became "crystallized." At some point, the magma from volcanic eruptions would carry these diamond crystals to surface where they could be mined. In uncut form, diamonds look dull and opaque. But in the hands of diamond cutters and master jewelers and after the cutting and polishing and with the exterior facade stripped away, they become the sparkling and brilliant beauty that they are. That's when diamond's "beauty from within" finally reveals itself.

I also see the same process that reveals this quality in a lot of our cancer patients. Most came to us with the initial shock or numbness from the diagnosis which quickly transformed into various stages of coping mechanism: fear, anger, depression, withdrawal, and acceptance, in no specific order. Then came the surgery, chemotherapy, and or radiation and each would leave its own physical and emotional marks. I have seen these deep physical and emotional scars so many times and in so many years that I, too, become somewhat numb to them. Perhaps, this is my own coping mechanism (indifference) so I could be emotionally objective and stay in my practice. But what never ceases to amaze me is the "beauty from within" some of our patients have. Under tremendous pressure from the rigors of treatment and buried with shame, anxiety, or despair, somehow they find the courage to fight on and the grace to live as close to a normal life as they can. And for those with a stage 4 disease, facing a relentless enemy and mortality, they somehow find redemption in living one day at a time. What's remarkable is as the physical beauty being stripped away, they reveal the "inner beauty" that's clearly evident if you spend a moment talking to them. Many of them have faith in God and accept the ultimate outcome whatever that may be, even though they sometimes ask the question, "Why"?" They derive strength from the Heavenly Father who does not promise healing but promises peace. They have hope but also obedience in the path already mapped out for them. They have faith in us, the health care providers, sometimes more than we have faith in ourselves. They cherish simple moments with the ones they love. A beach trip with the family, a soccer game with a grandson, a wedding of a daughter, a high school graduation of a son, an evening-in-the-park concert, a movie date, etc. become monumental goals, perhaps because they know more than anyone else that the most precious moments in life are the simple ones spent with those they love and there is no promise for tomorrow. They fight and live because they know that everything in life is a gift not to be taken for granted. They face the enemy not always for themselves but more often for the ones they feel privileged to call family and friends. And to us, the health care providers, there is nothing professionally more privileged than to be a part of these patients' journeys and to witness the "beauty from within" revealed through their most pressured and ardent circumstances. They are our heroes and we admire their beauty.

Image by EWAR from Pixabay

"People are like stained-glass windows. They sparkle and shine when the sun is out, but when the darkness sets in, their true beauty is revealed only if there is a light from within."

– Elisabeth Kubler-Ross

Broken Formation

Migratory birds flying in V-shape formation can travel thousands of miles each year to their destinations. The V-shape pattern allows them to save energy as they traverse great distances, climb over high mountains, and cross vast oceans. The wind vortex created by the leading bird's wing tips creates an updraft behind and to its sides that gives the following birds on each side a lift and thus conserves their energy. They seem to care for each other and they take turns being the leader, so together as a flock they have the endurance to accomplish one of the most amazing feats of all God's creations. Flapping their wings not in unison but at different speeds and positions at the precise moments, they take advantage of aerodynamic efficiency for their journeys. But their flights are not without perils. They have to combat the elements and can die from complications of a suppressed immune system. I read that roughly 5 percent of the adult winter geese and 50 percent of their youngs will not survive their journeys and will fall out of formation.

We lost one of our leukemia patients at Crestwood hospital oncology unit (in Huntsville, Alabama) this week. She was a beautiful young woman who had worked tirelessly as a single parent of two. Able to fight off the onslaught of leukemia two years ago, she began to put the pieces of her life together and was making plans for her daughter's wedding next spring. Just as life was giving her a second chance, the dreaded disease returned with an angry vengeance. With the same courage and grace and tenacity as the first time, she again endured bouts of chemotherapy without success. The last treatment weakened her immune system so much that she succumbed to infections.

Being the mother goose for most of her adult life and leading her children through their journeys, she was always at the tip of their V formation. Physically and emotionally weary from her battles against leukemia, however, she fell back and relied on the "updraft" from her mother, daughter, friends, and the nursing and ancillary staff that cared for her to continue her life journey. They were there in her momentary triumphs and always there in her darkest hours. Her daughter and mother took turns to lead the flock. She derived pleasure in continuing to plan for her daughter's wedding and in splurging on some of life's greatest sins … cupcakes and chocolate!

Yesterday, my patient's family life flight formation was forever changed. Too weak to continue, she broke off from the flock and trailed off into the sunset. She fell from the V formation onto the loving arms of God.

Heather (patient's daughter), you are a young woman with such strength and maturity that undoubtedly come from your mother. Your faith in God and love for your family are all but evident to us, the health care professionals, as you constantly sat and slept by your mother's side during her greatest storms. Those are the moments that she needed your strength to give her the needed lift. In the coming days, when the condolences have waned and in the still of the night when the pain is most searing, just remember that her spirit is in you and the God you trust is always by your side as He has always been all your life. Your mother would want you to celebrate life and love and soar in your own formation as your wedding day approaches. Miss Hope (patient's mother), you have been and will always be the matriarch of your family. I cannot fathom the depth of pain in your heart when you lost both your father and daughter just two weeks apart from leukemia, in the month that we're to raise awareness and commemorate patients of this dreaded disease. But you faced adversity with your own grace, dignity, and with the faith that moved us all. To both of you, though I never could promise that we could overcome your mother's/daughter's leukemia, there is one promise I can now make. I promise there will be a day that Faith (patient) will rejoin your flight formation. On that day and from the other side of the horizon, you all will soar with joy as there will no longer be any storms nor tears nor suffering nor leukemia nor death. The updraft from each of you will again lift each other up and at the tip of the V formation is Jesus Himself and His updraft will lift us all up. God loves you and may God bless you always!

September 2016

Image by Manfred Antranias from Pixabay

"He will wipe every tears from their eyes. There will be no more death or mourning or crying or pain, for the old order of things has passed away."

– REVELATIONS 21:4, NIV

GOOD BYE TO A FRIEND

The greatest gift of being physicians is not the accolades that come with the profession nor the financial rewards that might come with our works but the privilege of being placed in our patients' lives at their most vulnerable moments. Tonight I went to say goodbye to a dear friend who spent the better part of her adult life as a nurse, an educator, and an advocate for breast cancer early detection, the same disease that she herself battled. Driving to the funeral home, I prayed that God would be with me and more importantly, that He would be with her family during this incredibly difficult time as her departure from this life was unexpectedly premature. She had struggled with pain and confusion in her last few days. So I also prayed that I would find the words to comfort her family and that they would forgive me, her oncologist, for not being able to save her. As I walked through the front door, I quickly realized that God was already there. He was in the hearts of all of her loved ones who greeted and embraced me with grace and, obviously, forgiveness. I was the one who felt comforted tonight. As I quietly said goodbye to this beautiful friend who was so loved by so many in this community, I remembered her last words to me in her few moments of lucidity a day before she passed: "I love you! You're a true friend!"

Life is a journey and the richness of life is not measured by material wealth but by the amount of love one collected along the way. In that sense, I feel truly blessed and immensely rich tonight. Rest well, my friend! As your husband said it best, your life as a nurse was about "paying forward" with love and good deeds and your legacy was teaching others to do the same. I am a recipient of that legacy.

February 2017

"Sometimes you can't pay it back, so you just have to pay it forward."

– Randy Pausch

An Autumn Leaf
in Springtime

It withered and fell gently onto the water below and slowly got swept away by the current to a riverbank downstream. A journey that came too soon to this autumn leaf in springtime.

Not so long ago, it burst forth from a tiny bud on a young branch to welcome the arrival of spring. Amid the fanfare of songbirds and the explosion of brilliant blossoms that were fueled by the warm sunlight, it was promised a season of joy, growth, and fulfillment. But stricken by the cruel reality of life, this springtime leaf became sick, withered, and then prematurely fell. The river that sustained its life will now carry it to the final resting place. For this young leaf, autumn had come too soon. It looked just as beautiful if not more so than its contemporaries that were still green and full of life. But yesterday, broken and drained of vitality, it gave up its color and its spirit and fell off the tree of life and drifted away.

Her name was Sophia. We recently lost this young and lovely woman to leukemia from our care. She battled her illness with courage and grace. She endured the indignities from chemotherapy with great dignity. She had to grieve the sudden loss of her father just a few weeks before her own death. And yesterday morning, she was reunited with him. Through it all, she never questioned God why autumn came in her springtime. Perhaps she knew as many of us suspected all along that the question was not to be answered, at least not in this lifetime. Perhaps it's evil exercising its prerogative in a fallen world and perhaps God allows bad things to happen to good people for His divine purpose, but years of seeing young patients suffering and dying prematurely make me grow weary of quick and aesthetically pleasing answers such as ... God needs another angel for His throne, or God picks the most beautiful flowers for His garden, and so on. Statements like "God doesn't give us more than we can bear" aren't comforting in moments like these. Her mother who will have cried at two funerals in a matter of weeks has much to bear. Her young husband will have much to grieve in the coming days after the initial numbness wears thin. We will know the answer when we come face-to-face with God. For now, we Christians can find solace in the promise that in the afterlife, we will again be made whole and have an eternal dwelling in a place of perpetual joy and peace with our Creator. Her favorite song "All Is Well with My Soul" will be played at her funeral tomorrow. It was also her sentiment toward her Heavenly Father during her struggle with leukemia and a testament of her faith.

On the other side of the riverbank, the fallen leaf will be carefully picked up by His hands and lovingly placed on another tree, the heavenly tree of evergreen where spring is eternal and autumn never comes. This leaf will be brought back to life and be united with others that had gone before. This time, God Himself is the Guardian of this tree of eternal life and all ... will be well.

March 2017

"In this world you will have trouble. But take heart! I have overcome the world."

– JOHN 16:33, NIV

"For now we see only a reflection as in a mirror; then we shall see face to face."

– 1 CORINTHIANS 13:12, NIV

Facing the Giant

With a smooth stone collected from a nearby stream, David swung his sling and slew the Philistine giant and saved a nation. He had the boldness of youth, courage of a shepherd, faith stronger than the giant's might, and the assurance of God's power on his side. David knew as he stood in the valley facing his giant, while both armies were watching on the hills, that he would come home triumphantly.

Cancer patients also stand in their valleys and face their own giants daily. They have the love of God and support from their families and friends, but they have to fight the battles themselves and they're not guaranteed to come home triumphantly. They did not ask to be bold and courageous. They did not volunteer to face the giants. They do not have the assurance that God would deliver them from their enemies. As fate would have it, they are just thrust into the valley where the giants stand looming. And fight they must. They can hear the cheering and encouragement from us, the health care professionals or families or friends, but alone they must fight. They have to pick up their stones and sling them with all the strength they have. Unlike David who quickly defeated his giant with one well-placed slingshot and with the intervening power of God, cancer patients' battles often rage on. Each battle looks different from the last but from the hills overlooking the valley, one can see them fight with fear or with faith and often with dignity and grace. They kneel and pray for deliverance but soon they have to stand and face their nemeses. They will fall and they will try to get up. They may retreat with haste at sunset but when the morning comes, they charge at the giants with whatever stones they have in hands. They are bruised, cut, and burned in their battles but they will do their best to hide the scars and regain some semblance of their former physical selves. At one time or another, they can be seen wiping their own tears so they can stare down their enemies. With each stone they pick up from the battleground, there is hope of success but never assurance. And that … is the reality of Davids and Goliaths in the oncology world. In our world, sometimes David wins and sometimes Goliath does. I don't know why that is and I find myself asking the same question for almost three decades, standing on a hill watching and cheering on many modern-day Davids. I can only surmise that we live in a fallen world and evil can win and God intervenes when it's in His will. I do know that God also sent His only Son to earth to face our many giants. In the end, the Son lost His earthly battle to the giants of the day but was raised from death and went home to heaven with a crown of victory and consequently saved mankind for an eternity. I find solace in the Jesus example that loss on earth can be victory in heaven.

There is one more thing I know. The cancer patients I see today are just as bold and courageous as David in biblical time. With hearts full of zeal for life and love for their families and heads held high, they will fight. And the God who helped David slay Goliath thousands of years ago will either help vanquish their enemies or carry their bodies home in His loving arms as He carried Jesus' over two thousand years ago. Either way, they are His beloved warriors. Either way, they are our heroes. And either way, the crowns of victory await them beyond the valley.

"You come against me with sword and spear and javelin, but I come against you in the name of the Lord Almighty."

– DAVID, 1 SAMUEL 17:45, NIV

Nurses Week

Nurses and nurse assistants wear many hats. They are greeters when patients are checked in. They are transporters when patients need to be wheeled back to their cars. They are cheerleaders when patients need a little encouragement. They are enforcers when enforcement can mean life and death. They are patients' best friends when they lend a shoulder for someone to cry on. They are counselors when patients come to them with a slew of psychosocial issues beside medical illnesses. They are teachers when doctors' orders need to be conveyed. They are students as every single patient is a unique human being who needs a tailored care. They are rescuers when vital signs signal deep trouble. They are comforters when the pain is unrelenting. They can be lifesavers when death hovers like a vulture. They are the first responders when code blue is called. They seldom take credit when a life is saved. But they double as clergymen to the patients' families when valiant attempts have failed. They are the waitresses when the request for coffee or soft drinks are made. They are the busboys when spills need to be cleaned up. They are the plumbers with Foley catheters in hands when bladders refuse to empty or miners armed with liquid explosives (and lubricated gloved fingers if necessary) when colonic contents become hard as coal and need disimpaction. And they do all that while holding their own bladders or bowels in check as sometimes they just don't have the time to take care of themselves. They are electricians when IV pumps and other electronic monitors throw a temper tantrum.

They are PR department when anger flares and complaints are hurled towards them. They are HR department when people call in sick and they have to scramble to pick up the slack. They are IT department when doctors are confused and need help on the hospital latest update on their electronic medical record system. They wipe the backsides of grandmas or grandpas to preserve whatever dignity there is left in them. They are happy faces when cancer is conquered and patients go home to start life anew. They are hand holders when that's all the medical profession can offer.

They are all of the above and more every day that they show up for work. They also can be seen praying with their patients as they recognize the ultimate Physician holds all the power. They sometimes are caught standing in a corner of a hospital and weeping quietly as all hopes are lost. And at the end of the day, there always is endless charting and shift change reporting as their families wait to see them coming home. But there is something nurses are not. They are not in it for fame nor fortune! For what they do, nurses and nurse's aides are too often underappreciated and underpaid. Nursing is more than a profession. It's a vocation. It represents the best of humanity. It is compassion for other fellow human beings who are infirmed, manifesting as selfless devotion to the patients' needs, often over their own. The world was, is, and always will be a better place because of nurses. Florence Nightingale, the mother of modern nursing, said it best: "The greatest heroes are those who do their duty in the daily grind of domestic affairs whilst the world whirls as a maddening dreidel."

Yes, nurses are heroes. Their patients know it. And the doctors who work with them know it too. Happy Nurses Week to all the nurses and nurse assistants! God bless you for what you are and what you do!

"Rather, ten times, die in the surf, heralding the way to a new world, than stand idly on the shore."

– Florence Nightingale

Graveyard Shift

One of the delights of making rounds in the early morning is to see these creatures slowly emerging from the nooks and crannies of the hospitals. They look tattered, sleepy-eyed, with hair that seems to have survived a cat-5 hurricane. The gals seem to wear remnants of their makeups from the previous day and the guys wear a 7:00 AM shadow. From the looks, you might think they've just come back from deployment to the middle-earth battles from the *Lord of the Rings* saga. They move slowly, yawn incessantly, and stop frequently to make sure they have all the i's dotted and the t's crossed before the morning report. And their breaths declare their preferred sources of caffeine—coffee or diet sodas. They are graveyard shift nurses and nurse assistants. I talked to them sometimes when I was on call and on occasions yelled at them (for reasons I don't remember ... probably for waking me up before the roosters crow). But I admire them and though they may not know, enjoy seeing them at the end of their shifts.

They are the ones who kiss their own children or other loved ones goodnight then head on to work as others come home from work. They are the ones who spend all night monitoring the vitals and ensuring the comfort of their patients while administering the scheduled meds and wake up the sleepy doctors when things go south. They call for code blue when things really go south and stay with the code until the endeavor is successful or clean up the aftermath if it's not. Either way, they will be an hour or more behind in their other responsibilities if that happens and more likely than not, they will have to stay later after the shift ends to make up for the time lost. Nursing is an honorable profession. Nursing is a perfect example of what it looks like when compassion, education, and dedication are combined. Graveyard shift nurses are all those plus more and that's the risk of anonymity ... the risk of being not seen or appreciated enough by other health care providers, hospital administrators, patients' families, and others.

Though not as often seen, I admire graveyard shift nurses and their assistants and I always enjoy seeing them at the end of their shifts. They look awesome even when they don't look their best! They don't look their best because they have left their best behind to care for their patients, for other health care providers, and for each other. In our world, they are the guardians of the galaxies when most of the celestial bodies go to sleep. They are the graveyard shift heroes!

"The guardians of the galaxies go to work when darkness descends and the graveyard shift begins."

– Author

Nurses' Hands

During one of the segments of the ABC television talk show *The View* in September 2015, one of the cohosts was critical of a beauty pageant, Miss Colorado Kelly Johnson, regarding the stethoscope around her neck when giving a monologue, describing her passion as a nurse. The comment rightly or wrongly received a wave of backlash from the nursing community. But truthfully, it is not the stethoscope that makes nurses and nurse assistants special. There are very few professions that demand more admiration and respect from me than nursing. And it is not their stethoscopes but their hands that set them apart from other professionals.

It is the hands of the ER nurses who help pull victims off the stretchers onto ER beds. It is their hands that promptly start IVs so lifesaving medications can be quickly administered among many other things they do. It is the hands of the ICU nurses that are placed over their patients' chests to frantically perform CPR or rhythmically squeeze the Ambu bag to deliver needed oxygen when "code blue" is called. It is their hands that, figuratively speaking, hang on to those who are falling off the cliff of life into the abyss of death and try to pull them back.

It is the hands of the oncology nurses that hold the hands of cancer patients to comfort them as chemotherapy is being infused. It is the hands of the pediatric nurses that rub the backs of the little ones who are sick and read them bedtime stories so that the parents can run home momentarily to take care of the siblings who are still well. It is the hands of the OB nurses that carry bundles of joy to place on the arms of ecstatic mothers. It is the hands of the neonatal ICU nurses who care for the preemies in incubators because without them, life is unsustainable. It is the hands of OR and Recovery nurses that allow surgeons to "heal" with "steel" (scalpels). It is the hands of surgical nurses that change bloody bandages and administer narcotics so postop patients can endure and recover. It is the hands of the medical nurses that drop their own lunches to respond to urgent demands from patients' family members, to disimpact severely constipated patients, or to discard human wastes in bedpans besides many other hats they wear. It is the hands of the grave-yard shift nurses that pick up the phones to call the MDs in the middle of the night because their patients just made a turn for the worse and get yelled at because someone's sleep is disturbed. It is the hands of the nurse assistants that wipe the backsides of someone's grandmothers not just because it's their job but also because it's their desire to preserve whatever little dignity left the grandmothers have. And when some soul departs this earth, it is the same hands that pay the last respect by clean-ing up the body before it's moved to the morgue or the funeral home. It is the same hands that help clean the hospital bed so in a few hours, they have the privilege of taking care of somebody else. And they do this day in and day out. It is likely the hands of the hospice nurses that stroke the hands of someone's parents as they're about to take the last breaths. It is likely the same hands that gently lower the eyelids to cover lifeless eyes so death looks a little more like sleep.

I have seen nurses standing in a corner somewhere in a hospi-tal quietly sobbing because their favorite patients just died. It is those times that their hands wiped their own tears and covered their own faces in anguish, perhaps partly because they somehow felt responsible for their patients' death.

If you have a chance to see Miss Colorado's monologue on YouTube about what it means to be a nurse, look at her hands. Her hands express her passion and purpose, not her stethoscope. Like any other nurse, more likely than not, her hands have touched, caressed, loved, comforted, carried, held, stroked, scrubbed, wiped, disimpacted, discarded, and I suspect on more than one occasion, wiped her own tears and covered the hopeless expression on her own face.

Yes, nursing is an honorable vocation because of nurses' hands. It is through their hands that their hearts speak.

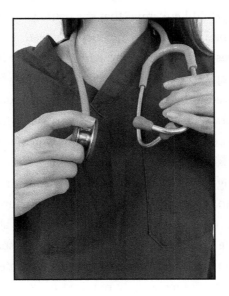

"The meaning of life is to find your gift. The purpose of life is to give it away."

– William Shakespeare

The Tenant of the Heart

S he was in her mid-twenties when she was pregnant with her second child. By the end of the second trimester, she learned that the AML (Acute Myeloid Leukemia) that she battled to achieve remission a few years ago had come back. The oncology team waited a bit longer to ensure she was well into the third trimester before initiating induction chemotherapy. The treatment went well but it wasn't long before the disease proved to be refractory. As more "reinduction" then "salvage" chemotherapy ensued, she became more pancytopenic and soon enough, daily blood and platelet transfusions were necessary to sustain her and her fetus' lives. Then came the frequent fever and chills leading to increasing number of antimicrobials from the ID (Infectious Disease) team to stave off the onslaught of opportunistic infections. Throughout the ordeal, her primary wish was to stay alive and healthy enough to ensure the delivery of her baby. Bone pain started to worsen, a combination of relentless leukemia and disseminated fungal infection. Pain meds were increasingly required to keep her comfortable. When it was clear that the treatment was to prolong the life of the mother to save that of the child, the OB team asked for the crash cart to be placed outside the hospital room so that in the event the patient was to code, resuscitation could be initiated to buy time for emergency C-section.

With the help of the Red Cross, her husband was able to come home from his overseas deployment to be with her through most of the treatment. As soon as it was feasible, she was induced to deliver ... a healthy baby girl.

She was transferred to the ICU for postpartum care but the menacing disease and the pregnancy by now had taken their tolls. Pain and rigors continued to progress and increasing doses of narcotics and sedatives were needed to keep her comfortable. Her husband would bring their newborn in to visit her daily and daily she was able to hold and rejoice in the growth of a new life as her own was fading.

She was made DNR (do not resuscitate) as the end was near. One night, the on-call oncologist was called for an order to place her on morphine drip as pain had become uncontrollable. A few hours later, the same oncologist was asked for another order to interrupt the morphine drip momentarily so her family could make one last visit.

Barely conscious, she embraced the baby as her husband placed it on her breasts. He leaned over and whispered in her ear: "It's OK, honey. We'll be OK. Don't stay for us. Go on home. We'll join you someday, I promise. We love you!" The grimace became a smile as a drop of tear formed at the corner of her eye. The rapid breathing abated and the pounding of her heart lessened. A moment later, the hands that tightly clutched the baby went limp. The cardiac monitor overhead that earlier displayed anguished, rapid gallops now showed occasional waves of agonal rhythm which gradually slowed to the eventual flat line as her soul departed. Outside the ICU of this small hospital in Southern California, the night was dark and the sky was starless.

I was the oncologist on call. It has been more than twenty years but

I remember this event as if it just happened last night. I was a young oncologist then, after just finishing my training at UCLA, and spiritually still wandering in the wilderness. I questioned the existence of God or His goodness in those days and this case didn't do much to convince me otherwise. I didn't think about this young mother much since that fateful night, perhaps because I wanted to keep the painful memory of her courageous battle suppressed, until now.

Recent signing to legalize abortions including full-term abortion in NY by governor Cuomo reminded me that despite the publicity and controversy regarding abortion, there are countless stories of mothers out there making personal sacrifices on a daily basis to ensure the safety and eventual delivery of their unborn babies that we don't hear about. They are willing to endure any suffering, cross any proverbial ocean, and climb the highest peak and lay down their lives if they must in exchange for those of the unborns. The tenants of their hearts are the lives of the ones growing in their wombs. It is unfathomable for them to do anything big or small that may jeopardize the arrival of the little ones into a world that is as ugly as it is beautiful.

So as we debate the issue of abortion, let's also pray for the mothers out there who are living and exemplifying the greatest of the human spirits: "Greater love has no one than this, than to lay down one's life for one's…."

I remember it was a dark night when this young mother took her last breath a long time ago. There have been many other dark nights since then. Nowadays, I try to look for the distant stars beyond the darkness of the night sky.

February 2019

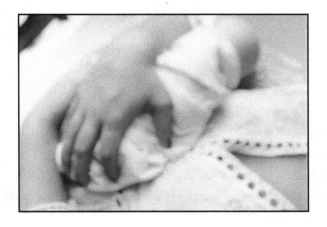

"All that I am, or hope to be, I owe to my angel mother."
– Abraham Lincoln

"Look into your mother's eyes and you will see a reflection of God's face."

– Author

TODAY

Today, the winter clouds were lifted and the sky declared the glory of God.

But today, a wife kissed her husband for the last time as his journey on earth just ended too soon in this hospital.

Today, the rainwater outside retreated and the debris of the streets were washed away.

But today in this ICU, a mother's hand stroked her young son's hair and caressed the body that was riddled by the marks of an overwhelming sepsis.

Today, the sun warmed the winter morning as if God's face was smiling on us.

But today, I held the soft hand of a beloved colleague to say goodbye and wished he had lived a little longer.

Today, the air outside was refreshing to the lungs and cleansing to the soul.

But today, sadness from the heart was billowing like the waves of a torrent sea in this hospital.

Today, churches all over Alabama preached the grace of God and the good news of salvation.

But today, I witnessed too much suffering before the homecoming of God's people.

Today, the message of "God does not give us more than we can bear" was proclaimed by a preacher or two.

But today, the burden was crushing for some as evidenced in the tears on their cheeks and the hidden pieces of their hearts.

Today, somewhere in these hospitals, someone questioned the goodness of God and the purpose of the suffering.

But today in these hospitals, before the tears ran dry and before the pain relented, "your will be done" was the ultimate submission in obedience. God is love and His grace abounds, even when we don't see it. I didn't see His grace in the ICUs, the medical wards, the emergency rooms or in the hallways of these hospitals today but I trust that it's there. It's always there!

February 2019

"For it is by grace you have been saved through faith."
– EPHESIANS 2:8, NIV

She Planted Her Flag

She cries like a lamb but will fight like a lioness the day she's told she has breast cancer. Part of what defines her physical beauty will be surgically "excised" because the enemy is growing in her. She tells her family she will be fine, but in her heart she is gripped with fear. The battle scar is soon carved across her chest even before she has a chance to really fight back. To face her enemy, she will endure months of "chemotherapy" that will make her sick and bald. To fight her giant, she will let "radiation" excoriate her body and scar her more than skin-deep. Then whatever is left that makes her soft and feminine will be removed by "hormonal therapy." She now feels less than a woman and intimacy is more of an act than a desire. If she's lucky, her partner will be by her side no matter what. If she's unlucky, this is about when her "partner" will bail out on her. Suffering all that, but day in and day out she will get up every morning—adorning her headdress as her helmet and her prosthesis as her breastplate—she will plant her flag and raise her sword to face her enemy.

Her body is weak, her stomach churning, her joints are stiff, and her muscles are sore but she will make her stand because she wants to live. She wants to live because she would love to share her tears as her daughter walks down the church aisle in a wedding dress, or at least to hear her daughter give the valedictorian address at the high school graduation or at the very least, to see her on stage at the … fifth-grade play.

She stages her fight during the day but it's at night that she is most vulnerable. It is in darkness and when alone that her enemy's greatest allies—fear, doubt, shame, depression, and despair—will likely forge their relentless attack. She is Joan of Arc to her friends and Mother Teresa to her family during the day, but when the night falls, alone in her bed, she is a weeping mess.

Then as dawn comes, she will rise up and stand. She will plant her flag and unsheathe her sword and stand her ground.

If the battle is won, she will rejoice with both laughter and tears … until the next doctor's visit, that is. If the news is good, she will make up for lost time and fill her days by loving and caring for her family and friends. If the news is not good, she will dust off her wig, replant her flag, and unsheathe her sword to again face her ever growing giant. This is a story of a breast cancer warrior but it's a story that's repeated a few thousand times each year across this nation.

October is breast cancer awareness month. It is also the month to commemorate those who valiantly fought this dreaded disease and cheer on those who are courageously fighting it now. This is the month we need to tell these breast cancer warriors that they are indeed our unsung heroes. They need to know that though we wish never having to fight this battle, if we do, we would want to have the same courage they have. They need to know that they looked beautiful the day they were diagnosed with breast cancer. But on the day they fought their last battle, standing with their flags planted by their sides and their swords unsheathed, and though they may have been bloodied, mutilated, and burned, they looked even more beautiful then. They planted their flags and wielded their swords but it is their hearts that won the battle. October is all about them, because they have fought and earned it! God bless them all this October and God bless them all every month thenceforth!

Image by bonoflex from Pixabay

"You cannot swim for new horizons until you have courage to lose sight of the shore."

– William Faulkner

CHAPTER 9

MY HOME FIELD

Journey Home

O ur friend from church went home with the Lord last night. No matter how much we wanted him to stay a while longer, his life journey was completed. He left us too soon but as Christians, we're comforted by the knowledge that as he took his last breath on earth, he breathed his first in heaven and as he slipped away from the loving arms of his bride and family, he fell onto the loving arms of God.

Someone has said that we are "spiritual beings having a human experience" so our earthly existence is meant to be temporary and on the day we're born, our journey home began. Most of us don't get to choose when the journey begins and when we arrive so we just ... travel on. What makes life journey so precious is not the green pastures nor the quiet waters along the way and definitely not the ups and downs nor the detours and the challenges but it is precious because we get to experience them with the love of our life by our side and family and friends nearby. With them, we cross vast oceans and climb to the mountain peaks from the deepest valleys. So when our friend crossed the divide last night and completed his journey early, how sorrowful it must have been for his wife and children and close friends. But they are strong and faithful people and they will travel on. They and we, as his friends from church, know that we will someday see him again.

Personally, I remember this friend who, for so many years, led me and my family to our seats in our church sanctuary as a volunteer usher. We tend to come in late to church services so the light was dimmed and the worship music already started but he patiently found enough seats for the entire family.

The next time I see him, I will look for his distinguished face with a pleasant smile to help me find my seat. There, in the sanctuary of heaven, we'll worship together. And there, in the bright light of heaven, we will see things more clearly and our unanswered questions will be answered by our Lord and Savior.

March 2016

"For now we see only a reflection as in a mirror; then we shall see face to face. Now I know in part; then I shall know fully, even as I am fully known."

– 1 CORINTHIANS 13:12, NIV

Slipping the Surly Bonds of Earth

John Gillespie Magee, Jr. was an American pilot who joined the Canadian Royal Air Force before the US entered WW II. During one of his flights in a Spitfire Mk I in August 1941, he climbed to 33,000 feet and the aerial experience was so ethereal that he later penned the words of a poem named "High Flight," which he included in a letter to his parents. Unfortunately, a few months later, the nineteen-year-old pilot died in a midair collision over the sky of Lincolnshire, England. The poem described exhilaration as an aviator and its words were so beautiful that it became immortalized in aviation history and were recited or inscribed in numerous aviation ceremonies and memorials:

> "Oh! I have slipped the surly bonds of earth
> And danced the skies on laughter-silvered wings;
> Sunward I climbed and joined the tumbling mirth
> Of sun-split clouds ... and done a hundred things
> You have not dreamed of.... Wheeled and soared and swung

High in the sunlit silence. Hov'ring there
I've chased the shouting wind along, and flung
My eager craft through footless halls of air....
Up, up the long, delirious, burning blue
I've topped the windswept heights with easy grace
Where never lark or even eagle flew....
And, while with silent, lifting mind I trod
The high untrespassed sanctity of space,
Put out my hand, and touched the face of God."

After the tragic loss of the space shuttle Challenger on January 28, 1986, one of the darkest moments in American aviation history, then-president Ronald Reagan gave a heartfelt remark which ended with, "We will never forget them, nor the last time we saw them this morning, as they prepared for the journey and waved goodbye and "'slipped the surly bonds of earth'" and "'touched the face of God.'""

Not being a pilot, I can only fathom how free it must feel to "slip the surly bonds of earth" or to break through the confinement of gravity and soar above the "sun-split clouds" and come face-to-face with the magnificent blue sky and feel God's face and how surreal it must feel to effortlessly glide to the distant horizon at dawn when the warm and radiant sun rays are beginning to brighten the sky or at dusk, when early stars are dancing across the heavens. And earth with all its splendor must be even more spectacular from above. I can only imagine that up there, in the silence and vastness of space and freedom from the distraction of earth, the majesty of God is more evident and His creation is even more appreciated.

But we don't have to be at lofty height to "touch the face of God." The most beautiful reality of life is God's presence right here, on earth.

It seems as though He prefers to dwell in our hearts over presiding in the heavens. So much so that He sent His one and only beloved Son to temporarily live and walk among us on earth, and suffered the consequences of our sins so we can be redeemed to walk with Him forever in heaven. He seems to care for all, especially the least among us. His face can often be seen in the faces of the sick children and of the poor and afflicted and the people who care for them. Touch the faces of one of these and you touch the face of God. "Whatever you do for the least of these, you do unto Me," He said in Matthew 25:4.

This morning, thousands were trying to do so by walking or running from 5K to full marathon in Memphis, Tennessee, to raise awareness and funds for St. Jude's Children Research Hospital. On the sideline to cheer them on was a little boy from Huntsville, Alabama, named Jacob Brown, my nephew, who is fighting leukemia and whose hand and heart were touched by the runners' act of compassion and generosity. For the rest of us, we should always try to be kind to one another, love each other, and be careful not to label each other unjustly. Most of all, we should reach out and help the poor and the sick. For doing so, we may temporarily "slip the surly bonds of earth" and "touch the face of God."

December 3, 2016

"Oh! I have slipped the surly bonds of earth …
Put out my hand and touched the face of God."

– John Gillespie Magee, Jr.

SHADOW ON THE WALL

I was only a few years old but I vividly remember the time when Qui Nhon, Vietnam, was hit by a great typhoon. For weeks, there was no electricity and the tsunami-sized waves had swept through the coastal city causing unimaginable carnage and death. The torrential rainstorm seemed to last forever and parts of our community were submerged under water while other parts were so badly flooded that we were imprisoned in our own homes. I remember peeking out the window at every daybreak and saw nothing but a wall of water coming down and the street outside had turned into a flowing river. At night, we huddled together around a candlelight after dinner and listened to our parents' childhood stories and occasional broadcasts on the radio amid the pelting rains and howling winds. The only other entertainment that I remember was playing "shadow on the wall." Provided by the dim light of a flickering candle, we used our hands to make shadowy figures on the wall and competed to see who created the most realistic and imaginative ones. The game seemed to give us a measure of joy and comfort at a time when the threat of death or destruction was just lurking outside. Perhaps it's because that's the only thing we could control in a world that we couldn't. It gave us peace in a scary and turbulent time.

The shadow moved as we moved and out of simple hand movements came some of the most entertaining artworks on the wall. Eventually, the storm subsided then stopped one morning. I stepped outside and the dreary sky gave way to a blue canvas with the most beautiful white clouds that were brilliantly outlined by a heavenly and redeeming sunlight. Yes, there were ruins all around us, but the brightness of the day brought promise for a new beginning.

We moved to Saigon and, years later, during the Tet offensive in 1973, our family and community were besieged by another life-changing event. But this time the carnage was caused not by a natural disaster but it was completely man-made. At the height of the Vietnam War, the North Vietnamese had come close to and in fact invaded parts of Saigon, then the capital city of South Vietnam. For weeks, the enemy leveled their cannons and even SAMs (surface-to-air missiles) from high grounds on civilian neighborhoods to inflict as much casualties as possible to break the South's will to fight. This time, the threat also came from above and as a young boy I learned that death and destruction could come randomly and instantly. I remember the familiar power outage and the familiar flickering candles at night and yes, the familiar shadows on the wall. But by the grace of God, we survived.

We all go through difficult trials in life and the scripture even promises this reality. We live in a fallen world where evil thrives and bad things happen to good people. But God also promises to be with us as we wade through the deep and difficult waters. Like the shadows on the wall, He is here to give us a measure of joy and comfort as we're going through the storms. He gives us peace in a turbulent world. He doesn't promise to deliver us from these storms, but He will give us what's necessary to weather them. Also like a shadow on the wall, He moves as we move and when our hearts break, His does as well. We are His priceless possession and He will move heavens and earth to be with us in our darkest hours.

Even if we are swept away and don't survive our calamities, whether it's tragedies or illnesses, God also promises those who know Him that He would wait for us on the other side of the "Jordan River," where we'll be with Him for an eternity. And that alone should be the source of joy and comfort in "all circumstances." Be well, my brothers and sisters! I'm praying for those of us who are suffering right now but I know you are closest to God now than ever. He is in you! And when in doubt, stretch out your hand and see His shadow on the wall.

"In His hand is the life of every creature and the breath of all mankind."

– JOB 12:10, NIV

A LIFE WELL LIVED

I remember seeing him on the side of a country road in the summer of 1988. This was one of the first times that I traveled to the heart of rural Alabama, the state that I come to love and now call home. He was a tall and ruggedly handsome man in his late forties—sporting a trucker cap and wearing a well-pressed long-sleeved shirt that's tucked inside a pair of neat blue jeans, complete with cowboy boots and a big buckle belt—standing by his fruit stand. His front shirt pocket was imprinted by a pack of cigarettes. The fruit stand was stacked with luscious watermelons, baskets of red tomatoes, Chilton county peaches, and bags of boiled peanuts. The midday sweltering heat didn't deter him from doing what he appeared to enjoy doing—waving, chatting, and selling his goods to drive-by customers. He stopped momentarily to greet me with a strong handshake, a stern smile, and a surprisingly warm, "How are you doing?"" After meeting my father-in-law for the first time, my newly-wed wife and I drove a few more miles down the winding roads, passing vast fields of various crops, a peach orchard or two, and the lush countryside that's punctuated by a few glistening ponds and herds of livestock before we arrived at his house, to be welcomed by his wife. It was a simple but rustic and lovely country home on a property completed with an old barn, a few pecan trees, and fenced-in billy goats. Down the road was a little garage that he apparently spent his spare time tinkering as a semiprofessional mechanic. For the next three decades that I knew him, the man they called "outlaw" was in my mind, the embodiment of the hardworking middle class America that loves God, country and family; the man I came to truly love, respect, and admire.

Born and raised in Alabama, he married his sweetheart a few years after high school. His family quickly grew to five with three beautiful children and a bride that he cherished until the end of his life. He was, I suppose, a typical blue-collar worker who lent his skills at a paper mill, a power plant or two, and numerous pipelines that crisscross the land, doing the type of works that form the heartbeats of our great nation. Later in life, he became a steward of the Teamsters local chapter and his work would often take him away from home, between pipelines and even movie sets. But home was always the Yellowhammer state where he dabbled in fruit stand business (in between "jobs") and that's where I first met him.

He taught those that knew him, including myself, the dignity of working hard with one's hands and earning one's wage by the sweats of the brows. He provided for his family with the conviction of an honest, honorable, and generous man. But hard times did befall his family early on in his career and I heard of stories of when he would go hungry to make sure his children had enough to eat. His character never changed in all the years that I knew him. Behind the tough exterior was a gentle soul with a generous and tender heart that's evident in his work as much as in his home.

He still worked, giving advices to coworkers on his sickbed in the last few weeks of his life and this morning, surrounded by his wife and children and some grandchildren, he took the last breath on the land that has been in his family for generations.

I always think that the measure of a man's wealth is not how much he owns but how much he's loved and today, he left this life as a very rich man indeed.

Because of him, every time I see a fruit stand by a country road, I see such beauty in the type of work that's seemingly humble and yet so respectable. Because of him, every time I pass a trucker on a highway, I do so with such care and respect that he deserves. Because of him, whenever I hear of a crew working on the pipeline or a movie set, I think of the diversity that makes America great. Because of him, the Teamsters to me means fair and honest workers that form the backbone of a productive nation. Most of all because of him, I realize that sacrificing for one's family is the virtue of a truly great man.

Sleep well, Mr. James Marion Traywick! Thank you for a life well lived and the lessons you left behind! I will see you on the other side of the river someday. Until that day, I will miss seeing you. One of my greatest honors in life is to be your son-in-law. You were a loving father to my wife, a wonderful "paw paw" to my children, and a personal hero of mine. I love you, sir!

April 2017

"That man is a success who has lived well, laughed often, and loved much."

– Robert Louis Stevenson

PRECIOUS GIFTS

I remember learning my first English word from my mother as she just learned the word herself. I remember watching my mother, in a heavy Vietnamese accent, asking the manager of Piggly Wiggly where she worked, if she could get a job application for me, a high school student and an immigrant's son in South Carolina. I didn't get the job but to this day, I still appreciate her noble attempt. I remember one cold winter morning, my father drove to my college campus in Charleston, South Carolina, in his pajama to help jump start my stranded vehicle. I remember seeing through the rearview mirror my mother's tears as she stood watching me driving away to Louisiana for my internship. I remember the first date with a nurse at Charity Hospital in New Orleans and my heart was gripped with joy—and nervousness. I remember the happiest day of my life as we tied the knot a few months later during our lunch break, in the courthouse a block or so away from where we worked. I remember six years later holding my daughter for the first time in Anaheim, California, and felt another kind of love that I didn't know I could have. I remember the sweet voices of my toddler sons in Huntsville, Alabama, calling me on my cell phone and asking what time I would be home so that they could see me before they went to bed. And there were countless moments on the bleachers cheering for our children on the ball fields or volleyball courts. I remember telling my dying friend that his Heavenly Father was waiting for him on the other side and saw his grimace turn to a smile. I remember my nephew Jacob—in the midst of fighting leukemia, when he turned ten—wishing that he would not be given gifts for himself but our family would buy Lego sets for his fellow St. Jude patients. I remember one night sitting in a New York apartment, holding my mother's hand for the last time as she lay mostly motionless from the stroke she sustained some years earlier, and she looked at me with the familiar tears from her eyes. I realized then that after all these years, and after all the places that my career brought me to, her love and concern for me never waned.

We all had moments like these and they are undoubtedly the most memorable moments because they are snapshots of the times we spent with the people we love and care for most. Those that God put on our paths often are the most precious gifts in life. They say we came into this world with nothing and we will leave with nothing but I disagree. We came into this world with the love and predestination from our Heavenly Father and for most of us, the love and excitement from our earthly parents. And we will leave this world with the memories of what's most important in life. Before we take our last breath, in the twilight between this world and the next, it's possible that what will replay in our soul will be the best memories of our lives.

Yes there are memories of hardship and heartbreaks too. But as light can conquer darkness, love can and will ... heal brokenness.

The scripture says, "Every good and perfect gift is from above, from the Father of the heavenly lights, who does not change like shifting shadows." Indeed, these wonderful moments of our lives are good and perfect gifts from God.

There is no better way to return God's favor than allowing ourselves to be used as His gifts to someone else. As flawed as we are, at the right moment, and with our willingness to give of ourselves and with the right words or actions, we can make a difference in someone's life as so many have done so in ours.

"Every good and perfect gift is from above, from the Father of the heavenly lights, who does not change like shifting shadows."

– James 1:17, NIV

My Childhood Home

This is my childhood home (the one in the middle of the photo shown). My brother Vinh took this photograph in 2016, when he came back to Saigon (now Ho Chi Minh city), Vietnam, for a visit. I grew up in a family of eight in this house. At one point, there were twelve of us as my aunt and her three children needed a place to live. It hasn't changed since I and my family left Vietnam in 1975. It is about 1,000 square feet. It has a small living room, two bedrooms, a kitchen, and one bathroom that we all shared. I learned my first English word here from my mother, a teacher. I learned how to ride a bicycle (that my dad bought "used" from someone) on the street where this house sits. I remember at the age of nine, my younger brother and I filled sandbags right outside the green metal sliding front door so my family could build a makeshift "bunker" inside one of the bedrooms. This is during the Tet offensive in 1968, at the height of the Vietnam War when the North Vietnamese communist forces invaded the South and came within miles of my home. We withstood nightly artillery shellings by sleeping inside the bunker. We survived!

Seeing this photo and looking back, I am the way I am and where

I am today is all thanks to God's prevenient grace. I am the one He left (temporarily) the ninety-nine for. I love my heritage. I love America. I love my current home state, Alabama. I love my family and friends. And I love the One who sought and saved me.

My story maybe different from yours but the God who seeks you out is the same One who rescued me. It is in the darkest hours of our lives that He fought the hardest for us. It is when we're weak that His strength is sufficient. Even when we doubt, He still believes in us. Even when we break His heart, His longing for us is unbroken. Even when we turn our backs, His eyes still cast a loving gaze. Our lives may not be perfect but His love for us is.

Someday I will go back and find this house. It is part of my childhood and I am grateful to my parents for the childhood I had. And I am grateful to my Heavenly Father for my privileged life. Someday, you and I will move to a permanent home in heaven. Until such time, we have much work to do here on earth, my friends. There is so much darkness on this planet that we call home. As long as we're here on earth, let us be the light it needs. Let's seek to do good whenever we can. We are all flawed, but we can reflect the light from the One who is flawless.

Photo by Vinh Dang. Used with permission.

"Therefore I will boast all the more gladly about my weakness, so that Christ's power may rest on me."

— 2 Corinthians 12:9, NIV

TRUE ALABAMIANS

You're from Alabama if:

- You believe there are only two seasons: college football season and the rest of the year.
- Your third favorite holiday of the year is Iron Bowl.
- The only proper greetings are "roll tide" or "war eagle" (you may want to add another word, "roll," as in RTR or insert the word "damn" as in WDE if you really mean it).
- You wish that Santa would place a 12-gauge double barrel under the Christmas tree and fill your stocking with 00 buckshots this year.
- Your favorite beverage is sweet ice tea. Favorite appetizer is fried green tomatoes. Favorite entree is fried chicken. Favorite side is fried okra. Favorite dessert is fried bananas with a scoop of fried ice cream.
- Your favorite vehicle to drive to work is a truck. Favorite vehicle to go to Walmart is a truck. Favorite vehicle to drive to church is the same truck.

- You drive to the countryside to look for cotton fields and experience a "white Christmas" that lasts more than just a day.
- Your favorite Christmas song is "Grandma Got Run Over by a Reindeer."
- Your favorite fish is the catfish that swims three times in its life: once in the Tennessee River, once on the frying pan, and once in your stomach.
- When away from home, you feel homesick when the band Lynyrd Skynyrd plays its classic "Sweet Home Alabama" on the radio.

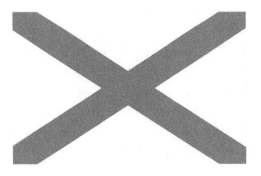

"Why would you want to marry me for, anyhow? So I can kiss you anytime I want."

– Melanie and Jake, from the movie
Sweet Home Alabama

FIGHTING A GOOD FIGHT

Jacob Brown (my nephew) was diagnosed with ALL (acute lympho-
blastic leukemia) at the age of nine and has been a patient of St. Jude
Children Research Hospital since. When he turned ten, Jacob asked
that instead of birthday gifts, his friends and family would buy LEGO
sets to donate to the St. Jude affiliate clinic in Huntsville, Alabama, so
other patients can play with them while waiting for their treatments.
An avid hockey player, Jacob is also the honorary captain of Huntsville
professional hockey team, the Havoc. Jacob received weekly chemotherapy but he would regularly get on the ice with his "teammates"
prior to the games during their season. I remember one night, a few
months ago, Jacob was treated in the ER of Huntsville Women and
Children Hospital for neutropenic fever and the next night, he skated
out during the introduction of his teammates prior to their game and
stayed long after the end to help auction their jerseys to raise funds for
a charity. The Havoc organization and their players are indeed an asset
to Huntsville. They regularly work on and off the ice to raise funds for
various charities including that for St. Jude. They exemplify not just
what's good but also what's noble about sports.

This week, the Havoc ended their season by winning the President's
Cup, the championship of the Southern Professional Hockey League,

after beating the top-seeded team from Illinois. This week, at the age of eleven, Jacob helped hoist the coveted President's Cup on the ice that his heroes and friends had just won while wearing a fake beard to support his team (apparently it's not uncommon for hockey players to grow beards during playoffs as a superstitious ritual). This week, his teammates honored Jacob, their hero and honorary captain, by letting Jacob touch the cup first before anyone else would.

Sports is not just about winning but more importantly about fighting a good fight and honoring each other. In life and in sports, Jacob demonstrates the best of the human spirit. Thank you, Jacob and the Havoc hockey team for bringing glory and humanity in charity to Huntsville, Alabama, and the hockey community as a whole!

April 2018

"I have fought the good fight. I have finished the race. I have kept the faith."

– 2 Timothy 4:7, NIV

I Am My Father's Son

I remember when you took me on bicycle rides after you came home from work. I must have been three or four years old then. I remember you showering me with gifts when I did well in first grade. I remember the Tet offensive when our family huddled in a bunker each night to survive the enemy's shelling. I remember the day you took our family from home and escaped to America as the communist forces were closing in. I remember you working different jobs in the early days as an immigrant so we could start a new life in the land of freedom. I remember, as a high school student in a new culture, I would throw away the meal tickets (for underprivileged students) and skipped lunch because I felt privileged enough just to be there. I would rather go hungry than accept the meals that I couldn't pay for. I never told you that but I believe I learned personal pride, self-reliance, and work ethics from you. I remember one early cold winter morning, you came to my rescue to jump start my stranded car on a college campus, wearing a jacket over your pajama. I remember many moments that we talked about life, family, and God as we rode together. I remember you brimming with pride when I was accepted to medical school.

I remember your excitement (and relief) when I finally got married, and the same excitement years later that showed in your voice whenever you asked about Karen and the kids over the phone. I remember how well you cared for Mom as her health was deteriorating. There are many memories between us that have faded but there are those that are indelibly etched in my soul. I have always been grateful to be your son. A perfect man you were not (but neither am I nor is anyone else I know) but a good father you always were. It is indeed the highest compliment that I can receive when I'm told that I am just like you. I am my father's son. My heart is heavy as you left to be with God today. But I am at peace that you no longer suffer. Tell Mom, my brother Quang, and sister Loan hello when you get to heaven. I love you! I will see you all on the other side. So long, Dad!

May 4, 2018

"Train up a child in the way he should go; even when he is old he will not depart from it."

– Proverbs 22:6, NIV

THE FINAL KISS

Several years ago, our family decided to scatter my mother's and my brother's ashes at sea. While doing some research on where and how to accomplish this task, I came across this story of a young widow who decided to scatter her husband's ash off their favorite beach.

They had vacationed together at this beach side community many times. They met and fell in love there and exchanged their vows on one beautiful early evening on this beach a few years prior. Under the deep blue sky and standing barefooted on the sugar-white sand, and with the rhythmic sound of the crashing waves in the background as their wedding chorus, they kissed for the first time as husband and wife. It was supposed to be the beginning of long and happy life together. Sadly, as fate would have it, the young man passed away unexpectedly a few years later.

So it was only fitting that this young widow wished to honor her late husband with a sea burial where they had so many lovely memories together. She chose one early evening, close to the hour they had married a few years earlier, but it's also when there wouldn't be many people on the beach as she wanted it to be a private event and she was also unsure how they would react if they saw what she wanted to do.

It was in late November and the water was frigid. The sky was outcast and the torrent sea was churned by strong winds into tall waves. It had rained earlier so the sand was cold and wet. She walked knee-deep into the water carefully holding the urn containing her husband's ash. She was gripped with an overwhelming sorrow and paralyzed by momentary hesitation but decided to push on. She kissed the urn one last time, opened the lid, then let the grainy white ash scatter in the wind. Suddenly, a strong gust changed direction and most of the ash was blown back onto her chest and face. She was stunned by what just had happened and her heart sank in dismay as the felt she had failed in her task. As the tears rolled down her cheeks, she felt an incredible sense of love and peace. She vividly felt at that moment the presence of her husband. The ash on her chest was his last embrace and what she felt on her cheeks was his kiss on them—for the last time!

She savored the moment as every bit of the ash fell gently from her into the water. As she looked up the clouds slightly separated, allowing a ray of sunshine to break through. It was a smile from heaven!

As she walked back to the beach, her spirit soared as she realized that her husband's last kiss on earth was his first promise of their reunion in the afterlife.

Friends, we all have grieved for the loved ones who went on before us. We all have our fair share of regrets about the things that we should or should not have said to them or about them or the times that we couldn't be with them. I know I have plenty. But we should be comforted by the knowledge that we'll have another chance. There will be a day that we'll be united with them and we'll have an eternity to right all wrongs and to make up for all lost times. God breathed life into dust and here we are. So to dust we must return but our spirit will also return to our Maker and there, we will dwell forever with Him and with our loved ones.

As for my family, on one beautiful sunny afternoon a few years ago, we took a boat to the harbor outside Charleston, SC, where my family settled and where I and my siblings grew up as immigrants from a distant land. As we scattered our mother's and brother's ashes into the calm water, I, too, felt a sense of closure and peace and hope of eventual reunion. Our God is a God of peace, love, redemption, and completion. From Him we come and to Him we will return.

August 2016

Image by Free-photos from Pixabay

"How did it happen that their lips came together? How does it happen that birds sing, that snow melts, that the rose unfolds, that the dawn whitens behind the stark shapes of trees on the quivering summit of the hill? A kiss, and all was said."

– Victor Hugo

A Little Old Lady in
Missouri

It was the summer of 1975. My family and I just escaped South Vietnam shortly before it was overrun by the communist forces. After a short stay in a refugee camp at a Marine base in California, we were sponsored by my father's friend who lived in Missouri. We stayed with them for about two weeks before my dad was offered a job in North Carolina. To this day, I'm not sure how he was able to scrape up enough money to purchase an old car for our journey east but he did. We stopped at a small restaurant somewhere in rural Missouri for lunch on the way to Charlotte. We—my parents and six children, of which I was the oldest (fifteen)—were the only customers besides a little old lady. She was by herself, sitting at a table close to us.

She glanced at us often, at least that's how I perceived through the corner of my eyes, always with a pleasant smile on her face. We must have looked pitiful, wearing pretty much the same clothes we left the old country in. We spoke only Vietnamese as my dad was the only one who could carry on a conversation in English. We ordered what we could afford from the menu but were all full when it was time to leave. The old lady left the restaurant some thirty minutes before we did. It was when my dad asked for the check that he was told the old lady had paid for our meal!

That was not the first time that my family was the recipient of kindness but it was the first time that I witnessed a random act of kindness from a total stranger who we only made eye contact from across a restaurant.

It was then that I first fell in love with little old ladies. I think of this particular old lady in Missouri often, especially when I'm called to donate my time or my resources for a good cause. They say we are products of the experiences we have with the people we cross paths in our life journeys. I'm grateful to this stranger in the summer of 1975 not just for her benevolence but for her part in shaping me the way I am. God often puts people in our paths to bless us or for us to bless them and sometimes the blessings are for a lifetime.

Image by PublicDomainPictures from Pixabay

"Kindness is the language which the deaf can hear and the blind can see."

– Mark Twain

Snowbirds and
Spring Breakers

My family and I go to Panama City Beach (PCB), Florida, for vacation often. Most of the times we went there in the summer, sometimes during spring break, but I think this weekend is the first time my wife and I go to PCB during February. We thought it would be mostly vacant and quiet but to our pleasant surprise, the place was crawling with snowbirds! In my humble opinion, there is only a slight difference between PCB in February when snowbirds abound and PCB in March when spring breakers arrive.

In March, the average age of PCB spring breakers is about the same as the amount of dollars they have in their bank accounts and in February, the average age of the snowbirds is roughly the same as the number of children, grandchildren, and great grandchildren they have, multiplied by ten.

In March, PCB is full of spring breakers trying to escape college and blow off some steam. In February, PCB is full of snowbirds trying to escape the frigid cold of the North and trying to get some steam back.

In March, college kids ride scooters up and down Front Beach road at all hours hollering at each other "What's up!" or with some unintelligible sounds. In February, snowbirds ride up and down Front Beach road in their white Cadillac from 11:00 AM to 5:00 PM quietly nodding at each other like, *I'm glad to be up.*

In March, guys walk up and down the beach wearing trendy swim trunks while gals strut in the opposite direction wearing the smallest bikinis legally allowed. In February, guys walk up and down the beach wearing baggy jeans and the thickest jackets legally allowed while holding the hands of gals wearing... the same things.

In March, spring breakers are spotted wearing cool 10-dollar sunglasses and holding five-dollar stale beers in their hands in PCB. In February, snowbirds are spotted wearing uncool 1,000-dollar bifocals and holding 2-dollar cups of vintage Chardonnay or Cabernet Sauvignon in their hands.

In March, college kids are seen doing the "crunk" or the "humpty dance" at PCB local bars and grills to the pulsating beats of pop music. In February, snowbirds already warmed up the places with slow dance to the not-so-pulsating beats of Hank William or Merle Haggard.

In March, crop duster planes fly up and down the PCB beach carrying banners with alluring messages like "Alvin's Island" or "Buy one get one free T shirts." In February, those planes are still in hangars and the only banners seen are hung proudly at some pharmacies with less than alluring messages like "Geritol" or "Osteo Bi-Flex."

In March, gals at PCB would buy t-shirts embroiled with the words "I'm hot" and know the words are figurative. In February, the gals who buy the shirts know the words can be literal at times. In March, the guys who buy the t-shirts spray-painted with the word "stud" are convinced that the shirts are made just for them. In February, guys who looked at the same shirts bought them some fifty years ago.

In March, you will occasionally see spring breakers use their cell phones to text their parents asking for emergency funds as they've overdrawn their allowances. In February, snowbirds occasionally use their cell phones to send emergency funds to the future spring breakers.

So today, I thought to myself that I was younger and cooler than most of these snowbirds. As I walked past the glass door of a bar and grill at PCB that played Hank Williams music, I saw the reflection of myself, wearing baggy jeans, a thick jacket, trifocal, and holding a glass of you-know-what! Oh well, my age has caught up with me faster than I thought. The only saving grace is my wife looks young and is as beautiful as the day I first met her. Tomorrow, I will need to change my image by going to Alvin's Island and look for that t-shirt.

February 2016

"Getting old is no problem. You just have to live long enough."

– Groucho Marx

EPILOGUE

In the final scene of the movie *Gladiator*, Maximus slays his antagonist, the evil and self-proclaimed Emperor Commodus but he himself has been mortally wounded. As his soul begins to depart the earthly body, he sees a wooden gate which he opens to reveal a mansion at a distance. He again finds himself walking through the wheat field. And when he gets to the other side of the field, he sees his beautiful wife and young son standing, waiting. With a lovely smile and a nod, his wife signals the young boy to run to his dad. Maximus is finally home!

Someday, we will walk through this gate and this field. On the other side is a mansion and across from the field are the loved ones who stand waiting to see us.

"Imagine where you will be and it will be so," Maximus encourages his men as they are about to face their last battle at the beginning of the movie. For those of us who are Christians, we have been promised in the scripture that the place God has prepared for us in our homecoming is so magnificent that "no eye has seen, no ear has heard, no heart has imagined" and in return, "Well done, my good and faithful servant" is what we would love to hear when we have crossed the fields of life and finally arrived home.

ACKNOWLEDGMENT

I would like to thank my wife Karen and our children Emily, Mark, Blake, and Tray for their love and support on this project. They are the winds that allow my sail to open on uncharted waters of this venture. Thank you to my colleagues, staff, numerous other healthcare providers, and most of all our patients for their faith and courage as we travel on our medical "field" and face many opposing "Goliaths" together. They are the sources of light that illuminate the paths in this sometimes cold, dark, and confusing world. Thank you to the missionary giants who sacrifice much of their lives and face countless challenges to lift the lives of others out of poverty, abandonment, and from other evils of the world and share the love and hope in Jesus. Part of this book is inspired by and dedicated to them. They are (in no particular order) Teresa June Estes of Desert Rose Ministries; Brad Jenkins of Until They Know Ministry; Steve James, Curtis, and Devry Coghlan of Kenya Relief; Steve and Leigh Willhelm of Project Abundant Life; and Chaplain Bessie White of Bessong & Ministries, Inc. Those are the few I know—among many other missionaries and evangelists out there—who are worthy of our praises and the Kingdom's crowns. Last and foremost, I would like to thank my Lord and Savior Jesus for my salvation, the Holy Spirit who gave me the words that I didn't have, and Father God for allowing me to fail in life at times so I can learn and grow to trust Him more, and to succeed at times so I can bless myself and others in His glory.

References

Brother Lawrence & Frank Laubach, *Practicing His Presence* (The SeedSowers, 1973).

May Patterson, *Seeking a familiar Face* (Exploration Press, 2017).

C.S. Lewis, *Mere Christianity and The Screwtape Letters, Complete In One Volume*, (HarperSanFrancisco, 2003).

Max Lucado, *A Love Worth Giving* (W Publishing Group, 2002).

Bruce W. Martin, *Desperate for Hope* (Baker Publishing Group, 2012).

Mother Teresa, *Mother Teresa: Come Be My Light: The Private Writings of the Saint of Calcutta* (Image. Doubleday, 2009).

Bob Goff, *Love Does: Discover a Secretly Incredible Life in an Ordinary World* (Thomas Nelson, 2012).

Ken Gire, *Windows of the Soul: Hearing God in the Everyday Moments of Your Life* (Zondervan, 2017)

Elisabeth Elliot, *Through Gates of Splendor* (Tyndale Momentum, Revised, Updated edition, July 2002)

Hacksaw Ridge (2016), Summit Entertainment

*Gladia*tor (2000), Scott Free Productions and Red Wagon
   Entertainment

Mulan (1998), Walt Disney Pictures

The Lion King (1994), Walt Disney Pictures

National Lampoon's Christmas Vacation (1989), Hughes
   Entertainment

Sweet Home Alabama (2002), Touchstone Pictures

Interstellar (2014), Legendary Pictures, Syncopy

Verses from the scripture (New International Version, English
   Standard Version, International Standard Version, and New
   American Standard Bible) are taken from YouVersion (also
   known as Bible.com or Bible App) version 8.11.1 by Life.
   Church.

Other historical and scientific information and famous quotes
   by notable people come from multiple sources including
   Wikipedia, brainyquote.com, etc.

CONSUMER DESCRIPTION

This is an inspirational book written from the perspective of a Christian cancer doctor, aimed to encourage and uplift us all who are caring for each other in the valleys among the fields of life. It also reminds us of the simple but most precious gifts in life and the need to care for those less fortunate than we are. Until we walk with God in His heavenly field, we are to walk with each other through the fields and valleys on earth.

CONSUMER SYNOPSIS

This is an inspirational book written from the perspective of a Christian cancer doctor, aimed to encourage and uplift us all who are caring for each other in the valleys among the fields of life. It also reminds us of the simple but most precious gifts on earth and hope for our eventual walk with God in His field in heaven.

CATALOG COPY

This is an inspirational book written from the perspective of a Christian cancer doctor, aimed at encouraging and uplifting us all who are caring for each other in the valleys among the fields of life. It also reminds us of the simple but most precious gifts in life and the need to care for those less fortunate than we are. Until we walk with God in His heavenly field, we are to walk with each other through the fields and valleys on earth.

Author Biography

M anh C. Dang, MD, author of the book *The Fields, Our Journey through Medicine, Mission, Life, and Faith*, is a medical oncologist at the Clearview Cancer Institute in Huntsville, Alabama. Manh is married to Karen and they have a daughter named Emily and triplet sons named Mark, Blake, and Tray. Aside from a busy oncology practice, Manh's passion is to work on the mission field, travel with his wife, dabble in photography, write inspirational Facebook posts, drive through the countryside at dawn, and go plinking when he can.

CPSIA information can be obtained
at www.ICGtesting.com
Printed in the USA
LVHW011134241219
641584LV00003B/3/P

9 781400 327768